LOVING &
OBEYING GOD

Books in the Woman's Workshop Series

Behold Your God: Studies on the Attributes of God
by Myrna Alexander
Designed by God: Studies on Healing and Wholeness
by Kirkie Morrissey
Faith: Studies on Living the Christian Life by Martha Hook
Forgiveness by Kirkie Morrissey
The Fruit of the Spirit: Studies on Galatians 5:22—23
by Sandi Swanson
Greater Love: Studies on Friendship by Jean Shaw
Growing Godly: Studies on Bible Women by Diane
Brummel Bloem
Heart Trouble: Studies on Christian Character by Barbara Bush
Loving and Obeying God: Studies on 1 Samuel
by Myrna Alexander
Mastering Motherhood by Barbara Bush
Open Up Your Life: Studies on Christian Hospitality
by Latayne C. Scott
Perfect In His Eyes: Studies on Self-Esteem
by Kay Marshall Strom
Talking With God: Studies on Prayer by Glaphré
Time, Talent, Things: Studies on Christian Stewardship
by Latayne C. Scott

Woman's Workshop Series

LOVING & OBEYING GOD

STUDIES ON 1 SAMUEL

MYRNA ALEXANDER

Lamplighter Books Grand Rapids, Michigan
Zondervan Publishing House

Loving and Obeying God: Studies on 1 Samuel
Copyright © 1982, by Myrna Alexander
All rights reserved

Previously published as After God's Heart: A Woman's Workshop on First Samuel
and A Woman's Workshop on Loving & Obeying God

Lamplighter Books are published by the Zondervan Publishing House
1415 Lake Drive, S.E., Grand Rapids, Michigan 49506

ISBN 0-310-37141-4

Edited by Evelyn Bence

Lady in the Garden by Claude Monet
Cover Photo by SUPERSTOCK INTERNATIONAL
Cover Design by The Church Art Works, Salem, Oregon

Printed in the United States of America

91   92   93 / CH / 14

to
our children,
David, Christina, and Jonathan,
who we pray
will desire
to be
After God's Heart

CONTENTS

PREFACE

As my eleven-year-old son, David, hungrily devoured an after-school snack, we discussed the events of his day. He told me how he had followed a particular rule, when those around him hadn't.

"Did the others laugh at you?" I asked.

"Well, sure," he casually replied.

"How did that make you feel?" I asked.

"Mom," he said, "I'd rather be a friend of God than anyone else."

This heart attitude, which cared more what God thought than what others thought, gripped me. Was being a friend of God the primary goal of my life?

Jesus said that knowing God is Life: "This is eternal life: that they may know you the only true God and Jesus Christ, whom you have sent" (John 17:3). Being a friend of God is what *living* is all about.

What makes someone a friend? A friend is concerned about what is important to her friend. Being God's friend means that I care about what is important to Him.

In the Bible God reveals what He thinks is important. Even the briefest look into the Scriptures shows that what God values often differs from what men and women see as valuable. We live in a society that praises externals and makes performance the criterion for success. In contrast, the Bible indicates that God is concerned with the *heart attitude* of an individual. The Bible summarizes it this way: "Man looks on the outward appearance, but the Lord looks on the heart" (1 Sam. 16:7).

The desire of God's heart is forcefully set forth in 1 Samuel 13:14: "The Lord has sought out a man after his own heart."

Today God is still looking for those with a heart attitude after His own: "The eyes of the Lord range throughout the earth to strengthen those whose hearts are fully committed to him" (2 Chron. 16:9).

Those of us who want to know God, who care about what is important to Him, must not take the matter of becoming after God's heart lightly. Yet in the quiet of our souls we wonder, "Lord, what does it mean to be after Your heart?"

God does not offer an abstract definition, but teaches us through a true story found in First Samuel. The Book of First Samuel is a historical narrative. In the Bible, narrative is never used for merely telling a good story; it has a larger purpose. Biblical narrative shows us God in action, and real people grappling with godly principles.

The narrative of First Samuel introduces us to individuals who come to know God and grow in faith by applying what they know about Him to their daily circumstances. We meet a woman named Hannah, who wanted a baby; Samuel, a young boy who grew up strong in the Lord, even though he lived in the midst of perversion; the warrior Jonathan, who chose to focus upon an all-powerful God rather than on military might; David, a teenager who, in the name of the Lord, faced a giant.

These are people who cared enough about God to follow His commands, and who became living definitions of what it is to be after God's heart.

But, not all the individuals in First Samuel cared about the things God thought important. Alongside the good models, we see what can hinder or even detour a heart attitude like God's.

Together we will discover that First Samuel is a very practical and encouraging book for one who desires that the Lord find her heart completely His. The challenge of God's Word is:

"Now devote your heart and soul to seeking the Lord your God" (1 Chron. 22:19).

ACKNOWLEDGMENTS

God often uses teams to accomplish His purposes. Surely this book is an example of this.

I am continually thankful for my husband's biblical scholarship, wise counsel, and constant encouragement in the study of the Scriptures. And the women in my Bible class who first studied this material also made an invaluable contribution. I thank all of them, and especially the class coordinator, Bonnie Paul, for their input and encouragement. I am also grateful for the faithfulness of Cheryl Comfort, who reviewed each lesson and offered many wise insights, and for the great encouragement of two excellent typists, Keeley Wright and Julie Vawser.

And finally, I am deeply grateful for the specific prayer support of family members, friends, and my church family.

HOW TO USE THIS BIBLE STUDY

This study was originally written for women who wanted to study the Bible together as a group, after having studied a passage on their own during the week. I believe that individual study is the key to group Bible studies where the goal is to see lives change. Great growth and personal encouragement took place in our group because we came together prepared by Scripture to interact on God's principles.

Effective study of the Bible involves commitment, and so this study guide requires consistent and serious study. However, the work is worthwhile, because it will result in fruitful and life-changing group discussions.

The lessons are intended to be done on a regular basis: one discovery section per day, one lesson per week. However, there is room for flexibility, according to the needs of the individual or group using the material.

Finally, it is my prayer that each person who uses these studies will come to know the joy and transforming growth in Christ that comes from daily studying God's Word.

SUGGESTIONS FOR LEADERS

The leader's primary goal is not to teach, but to lead a discussion in which the participants feel free to share discoveries from their own private study of the Bible. A wise leader can encourage learning by:

1. Trusting the Holy Spirit to work through her.
2. Providing a warm atmosphere where all are encouraged to share.
3. Keeping the discussion "on track," and not allowing it to go off on a tangent. The discussion should not be based on what people think, but on what the Word of God says. The lesson questions are designed to do just this. So the leader may always ask, "How did you answer the next question?"
4. Attempting to cover all the assigned passage and questions. This encourages the participants to finish the study.
5. Maintain the rule: only those who have finished the week's assignment may share in the discussion. What better way to encourage study?

6. Shortening or rephrasing the questions, when necessary, for the sake of time or interest.

7. Varying your method. Some questions will lend themselves to sharing around the circle, each woman giving part of the answer. At other times, an answer from one person may be sufficient. Or varied observations from several women may broaden the group's understanding.

8. Some groups find it helpful to have the leader summarize the lesson. Such a summary should include: making sure the biblical principles found in the current passage are properly understood (see the "Key Principles" section at the close of each lesson) and drawing applications that specifically relate to the group's needs.

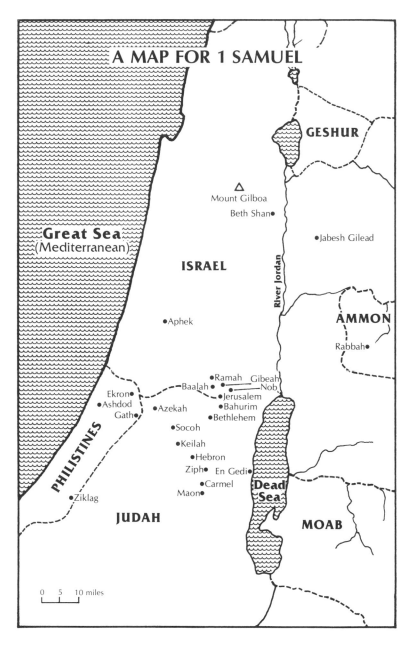

A MAP FOR 1 SAMUEL

Great Sea
(Mediterranean)

△
Mount Gilboa
Beth Shan●

GESHUR

●Jabesh Gilead

ISRAEL

River Jordan

●Aphek

AMMON

Rabbah●

●Ramah Gibeah
Baalah ● ●——Nob
Ekron● ●Jerusalem
●Ashdod ●Bahurim
Gath● ●Azekah ●Bethlehem

PHILISTINES

●Socoh

●Keilah

●Hebron
Ziph● En Gedi●

●Carmel
Maon●

Dead
Sea

●Ziklag

JUDAH

MOAB

0   5   10 miles

1

"I WANT TO BE AFTER GOD'S HEART"

Overview and Introduction

"Dear Lord, I've read and reread Your words: 'The LORD has sought out a man after his own heart. Man looks at the outward appearance, but the LORD looks at the heart' (1 Sam. 13:14; 16:7).

"Lord, I've begun to get to know You, to learn something of what You are like, and Lord, it seems precious to me—that You desire me to be after Your own heart.

"Yet to be honest Lord, I'm not exactly sure what this means. O Lord, would You mold my heart after Yours and show me Your truths?"

*   *   *   *

If this has been your prayer at one time or another, this Bible study is for you! And as we begin this study, let's not forget two of God's promises: "I will instruct you and teach you in the way you should go; I will counsel you and watch over you" (Ps. 32:8) and "Is anything too hard for the Lord?"

(Gen. 18:14). Together let us enter 1 Samuel and learn what it means to be after God's heart.

This lesson is designed quite differently from all the succeeding lessons. In order to more fully understand 1 Samuel, we will first look at the historical context of the book. Next we will grasp the book's overall perspective by reflecting on several chapters each day. By the end of the week you will have finished reading all of 1 Samuel. Such an overview will be valuable to you before digging into the truths of our narrative chapter by chapter, question by question.

Each day commit your study time to the Lord, ask Him to enable you to understand His Word and how it applies to your life.

Discovery 1 / Samuel's Place in History

1. Read the following background summary. Underline phrases and sentences you find particularly interesting.

2. Then answer the following questions:

   What was God's purpose for Abraham and his descendants, the children of Israel? In what way was Israel fulfilling or not fulfilling her purpose during the time of the judges?

   To make God known / Be a blessing
   Negatively — His discipline exhibited His power
   pull of Baal stronger than pull of God
   Sin appeared more attractive

   What epitaph was written over the years just prior to the events of 1 Samuel? What epitaph might you write for our day?

   Foolishness of man,
   Everyone did what was right (or wrong)
   in his own eyes.

The History of God's People

In the beginning, God warned Adam not to choose what looked right in his own eyes, but to follow God's instructions. However, Adam and Eve brought upon themselves the tragic consequences of choosing to go their own way, apart from God; fellowship with the Source of life was broken, seemingly forever. But God, full of compassion for His people, took the initiative to bring men and women back into relationship with Him.

God's plan to reconcile the world to Himself began with one man, Abraham. Through Abraham and his descendants God made a nation: Israel. Genesis 12 reveals that God called Abraham and his seed to be a blessing to the world. This "blessing" was ultimately fulfilled in the Messiah, Jesus Christ, but Abraham was also a blessing in his own time, as he drove his camels through the desert, as he stopped by an oasis for a drink, and as he greeted friends at the city gate. Whereever he was and with whatever he was doing, Abraham and his seed were called to this vocation.

God sent His people from Palestine into Egypt in order to keep them unified and so that they might carry out their calling of being a witness to Him. In Palestine, the Israelites were being drawn into the religious practices of their neighbors, the Canaanites. The Egyptians, on the other hand, were prejudiced against the Israelites and segregated themselves from them. By taking the Israelites to Egypt, God kept them a unified people rather than allowing them to become assimilated with the Canaanites. In approximately two hundred years the family of seventy grew into a nation of about twelve million.

For fear that they would be overrun by the Hebrews, the Egyptians made God's people their slaves. The oppressed Jews called out to their God, and He answered their cry by sending Moses to lead them out of bondage and back to the Promised Land.

The first five books of the Bible record the history of God's people from the call of Abraham to Moses' leading them to the edge of the Promised Land. This period of history was about six hundred years long.

The next period began when Israel, under the leadership of Joshua, entered the land God had promised to Abraham's descendants. This period, lasting about three hundred and sixty years and recorded in Joshua, Judges, and Ruth, started with victory for the descendants of those who had failed in their wilderness wanderings. This new generation trusted God to conquer this land through and for them.

In time, however, these enthusiastic followers of God made a tragic mistake. They did not fully carry out God's clear command and warning to drive the pagan inhabitants from the land. Enemy remnants gradually increased in number and strength, becoming a terror by night and day to later generations of Israelites.

The refusal of God's people to obey Him led them into other sad difficulties. Surrounded by the worship of many gods, the Israelites began overlooking the evils of paganism. "Accepting" the inhabitants of the land, they soon became influenced by pagan principles, intermarried, and then participated in idol worship. Eventually the Israelites who had worshiped God forsook His ways entirely!

Instead of the people of God pulling their neighbors toward Him the Baal worshipers pulled God's people toward Baal. God had warned Israel of this great danger. They became so involved with their idols that God, being faithful to His warning, withdrew His promised blessings. Because God loved His children very much, He disciplined them, so they might return to Him.

God's discipline of Israel came in the form of oppression; He used other nations to correct His people. This was a frustrating and sad period for the children of Israel.

During this time in Israel's history, no nation was powerful enough to control the entire Fertile Crescent area, as Egypt had in the past. Many smaller nations bordering Israel began to move in on her, at first as irritants, and later as destroyers.

Only when the situation became unbearable did the people in desperation turn to God. Then, in humility, they repented and began to follow His ways. But soon the pagan influences would again pull them away.

In the period of the Judges, this "cycle" occurred over and over again. The people would give in to their pleasure-seeking, selfish desires, caring little about God and His ways. Then God would discipline them through the pressures of other enemy nations who looted and destroyed their fields, businesses, and homes, until, in desperation, the people made tearful pleas for deliverance. God would then respond by raising up a "judge" as deliverer. (These judges included men such as Gideon and Samson.) But then, during the ensuing peace and prosperity, the people became lax, and soon they were lured back into idolatry. And so the cycle of: Sin—Sorrow—Supplication—Salvation—Sin recurred. Israel's continuing indulgence in pleasure and selfish desires dulled their love for God and lessened their respect for His authority, until God characterized them as follows: "Every man did what was right in his own eyes" (Judges 21:25 RSV).

This tragic summation concludes the book of Judges, which provides the immediate background to 1 and 2 Samuel.

An Introduction to 1 Samuel

The period between this spasmodic cycle of the judges and the establishment of a king in Israel is called the transition era. The actual "transition" involves the people moving from their dependence on God toward the leadership of men.

First Samuel covers approximately 115 years between the miraculous birth of Israel's last judge, Samuel, and the death of her first king, Saul. In recording the major events in the period, it reveals the very personal workings of God in the lives of individuals, notably three men called of God: Samuel, Saul, and David. Samuel is seen as a prophet, priest, and the last judge of Israel; he is the key figure in chapters 1–7. Saul, the first king of Israel, is shown as a man after man's heart; he is the key figure in chapters 8–15. And David, the greatest earthly king of Israel, is shown as a man after God's heart; he is the key figure in chapters 16–31.

First Samuel records the ways Samuel influenced the life of Israel and its leaders, the rise and fall of Saul, and the background for David's reign, which is recorded in 2 Samuel.

Who Wrote 1 Samuel and When

Many scholars hold that Samuel is the writer of at least some of this book, but another person or persons recorded the events after his death. The co-author of the book might have been one of the pupils from Samuel's school of the prophets or the priest Abiathar. (Abiathar fled to David when he was in exile after Saul massacred the priests of Nob.)

Discovery 2 / An Overview of Chapters 1–7

3. As you read 1 Samuel 1–7, note the following on the chart below:

   To help you remember the contents of the chapters, make up a descriptive title for each.

   Record under the "Insights" anything that seems important or anything you want to remember.

   Acquaint yourself with Samuel. Briefly list any observations you make concerning his character, noting the chapter and verse of findings. Be prepared to share these observations with your discussion group.

Chapter Title	Insights	Observations on Samuel
① Prayer Answered		Born/Dedicated
②	V 26	Jesus Luke 2:40 Can anything good
③ SAMUEL CALLED	in spite of surroundings	come From Nazareth Faithful
④ Fall of Eli	V 7-8	Knew God's reputation
⑤ Philistines + Ark		
⑥ Return of Ark		
⑦ Israel turns back to God		Judge

Discovery 3 / An Overview of Chapters 8–15

4. Read chapters 8–15 and fill in the following chart, as you did the chart in Discovery 2.

Chapter Title	Insights	Observations on Saul
⑧ Israel/King	Cost	Handsome
⑨ Saul chosen	Rule Book, for royalty	Tall Seemingly Humble (21)
⑩ Saul anointed/proclaimed king		Hiding
⑫ Coronation	God answers prayer	
⑬ Unlawful Sacrifice	people suffer consequences	arrogant/impatient

Discovery 4 / An Overview of Chapters 16–31

5. Read chapters 16–31, noting your titles, insights, and observations of David.

		Observations
Chapter Title	Insights	on David

_____

_____

_____

_____

_____

_____

_____

_____

_____

_____

_____

_____

_____

_____

_____

Discovery 5

6. Name three people in 1 Samuel who seemed godly. Give a reason for your choices by citing an example of their righteous attitude or actions.

   _____

   _____

   _____

7. Now that you have read through First Samuel, what do you think is meant by the phrase "after God's heart"?

   _____

   _____

2

COPING WITH HURT

1 Samuel 1–2:10

Pam sat across from me at lunch. It had been two weeks since her husband had moved out.

"I'm hurting!" she said. "I hurt inside! . . ."

"How can you expect me to think about God now?" she asked sharply. "I can't even cope with this hurt, much less God."

"Everyone tries to find relief from hurt," I said. "What relief have you found?"

"I've been grabbing at anything to stifle the pain," she answered. "A box of chocolate chip cookies, a shopping spree, complaining to a friend, even a relationship I know is wrong."

She was quiet for a moment, and then she looked at me very earnestly and said, "I'm a Christian now. What do you Christians have to offer me?"

*   *   *   *

Coping with hurt *is* difficult. We all seek relief when we're hurting. In this week's lesson we will discover practical—and yet biblical—helps for dealing with hurts and difficulties.

God begins the book of First Samuel by putting the spotlight on one family, and in particular, one member of that family. From this family would come a prophet who would model to Israel a heart after God, as well as hold that nation together in its darkest hour.

Cultural Insights

Polygamy: In Samuel's day polygamy was quite acceptable. In fact, it was almost the thing to do, since it was of supreme importance that one have descendants to carry on the family name. However, Scripture seems to imply that, for this time as well as for today, one wife is the ideal.*

Barrenness: In Old Testament times, it was a disgrace for a woman to be barren, and there were several reasons for this:

1. The Israelites were an agricultural society; so they needed to raise their own work force. Children, especially sons, were valued highly.
2. Sons carried on the family name and inheritance. This was of utmost importance. Men were also needed to protect the nation.

---

*The implication that one wife is the ideal is supported by—

1. the fact that God gave Adam one wife (Gen. 2);
2. the concept of oneness in marriage stated by God in Genesis 2:22–24;
3. the helper concept (Gen. 2:18, 21–22);
4. the fact that the king was not to take many wives (Deut. 17:15–17).

Levite: A member of the tribe of Levi. The patriarch Jacob had twelve sons. When Israel became a nation, the families of each of these sons became individual tribes. Each of these tribes had responsibilites in the nation. The tribe of Levi had been set apart of God to care for and administer holy things, for example, the temple and sacrifices.

Shiloh: A very important city of the nation of Israel in the time of Samuel, for it was Israel's religious center. It was centrally located to the twelve tribes of Israel. Later, Jerusalem served as both the political and religious capital.

Discovery 1 / A Godly Family—With a Hurt! / (1:1–6)

Israel is now at its lowest point, for "every man did what was right in his own eyes" (Judg. 21:25 RSV). God starts out the book by giving us a very personal glimpse into a family that is trying to reverence Him while living in the midst of a godless and immoral society.

1. Though idolatry was a sign of the times, what words and phrases give us some insight into how this family sought to be faithful to God? (See Exodus 23:15 and Deuteronomy 16:16 for some background.)

_____

_____

Look at v. 2. Though polygamy was culturally acceptable, in light of Genesis 2:18, 21–24 and Deut. 17:14–17 how might this have been a compromise with God's way?

_____

What evidence can you find of family problems in vv. 1–6?

_____

_____

_____

Can you think of any ways your family stands for God's ways in the face of pressures from modern society? Can you think of any ways your family is influenced by modern society to compromise God's principles? Try to be specific here.

_____

_____

_____

2. Though Elkanah was a God-fearing man, there was trouble in his household. What two problems was his wife Hannah dealing with? (vv. 4–7)

_____

_____

What phrase (used twice) in this discovery passage indicates who was responsible for Hannah's greatest disappointment? Though this may seem harsh or perhaps even unjust from our perspective, what help does Isaiah 55:8–9 offer us here? (Question 12 in this lesson may also help you.) (Note: Obedience to God does not guarantee a "problem-free" life.)

_____

_____

_____

Discovery 2 / A Stressful Situation / (1:7–18)

3. Read vv. 7–18 carefully and list any words or phrases that reveal or suggest emotions Hannah was experiencing as a result of her barrenness. For example, "Hannah was praying in her heart" shows a depth of emotion. Hannah is experiencing stress. She feels distressed.

   _____

   _____

   What other emotions might arise in this kind of situation?

   _____

   _____

4. How did Hannah cope with the situation described in this chapter? See vv. 9–10. (See also Philippians 4:6 and 1 Peter 5:7.)

   _____

   _____

   Which phrases in vv. 12, 15–16 reveal how important this approach was to her? What does this indicate about Hannah's heart attitude toward God?

   _____

   _____

   Can you identify any stressful situations at present in your own life? What principles might you develop from Hannah's approach to her problem that could help you? Be specific.

   _____

   _____

   _____

5. What means did the Lord use to encourage Hannah in the midst of her present distress? (v. 17)

_____

In what way might the Lord do the same for you in one of your stressful situations?

_____

_____

_____

6. What changes in Hannah could be noticed when she returned from the temple? (v. 18) What had made the difference?

_____

_____

What does our behavior tell about our faith? Can you think of a situation in your life in which you say "I am trusting God," yet your behavior and feelings don't show it? State it here briefly. What might your behavior be indicating? What could you do about this?

_____

_____

_____

_____

Discovery 3 / Faithfulness: God's and Hannah's / (1:19–28)

7. What phrases in vv. 19–20 tell of God's faithfulness to Hannah?

_____

_____

8. What course of action did both Elkanah and Hannah agree on in vv. 21–23?

_____

What does v. 22 tell us about Hannah's intention to be faithful to the promise she had made earlier to God?

_____

9. In your opinion, why might Hannah have wanted to stay behind with Samuel? Do you think it is good for a wife to make her wishes known to her husband? Explain.

_____

_____

10. In what specific ways did Hannah "take action" on what she believed God would have her do? (vv. 24–28) Has the Lord through His Word shown you something you should do? What is it?

_____

_____

_____

What action have you taken?

_____

_____

_____

Discoveries 4 & 5 / Hannah's Prayer / (2:1–10)

It is of great encouragement for us today to note that the years of suffering because of her barrenness and of living in a stressful home situation had made Hannah into a woman who knew her God. This comes through clearly in her prayer.

11. During the joyous yet perhaps difficult incident recorded
    in vv. 24–28, what does Hannah focus her attention on?
    Choose several phrases that you think best characterize
    her prayer.

    _____

    _____

    _____

    Choose several key phrases in this prayer that seem to be
    examples of God meeting Hannah's needs.

    _____

    _____

    What do Isaiah 26:3 and Psalm 9:10 add to our under-
    standing here?

    _____

    _____

12. Describe a difficulty you are presently facing.

    _____

    _____

    _____

    _____

    Select from Hannah's prayer three truths concerning God
    or what He can do in your present difficulty.

    _____

    _____

    _____

    _____

How do these specific truths apply to your present situation? Does this change your perspective of your circumstances in any way? How? Be prepared to share.

_____

_____

13. Challenge Question: In her great proclamation about God in vv. 1–10, Hannah also prophesied of that King in whom all Israel's hopes would be fulfilled, the Messiah. Where do you find that prophecy in her prayer?

_____

_____

Centuries later, but with a similar intensity, another young woman who was closely associated with this prophecy used the same themes to speak of the God she had come to know. Compare Hannah's prayer with the famous Magnificat of Mary (Luke 1:46–55). What themes are set forth in both prayers?

_____

_____

*   *   *   *

Key Principles from Lesson 2

1. God can use anyone. (chapter 1)
2. Principles for coping with hurt (1:9–16):
   a. Turn first to God for comfort, not to something or someone else. And give Him your emotions.
   b. Allow Him to encourage you, let *Him* choose the way.

3. Counsel and encouragement can come through God's spokesmen. (1:17)
4. When God shows you something you are to do, take action. (1:17–18)
5. In summary, in the circumstances of life, especially the difficult ones: (1) stop; (2) focus your attention on the Lord, His character, and His works; (3) apply these truths to your circumstances; and (4) live in the light of this application.

3

WHO OR WHAT IS MY AUTHORITY?

1 Samuel 2:11–3:21

As she was growing up, Karen had wanted to have her own way at home. And at school she'd found it hard to obey her teachers. Later, as a wife, she found it very difficult to submit to her husband's leadership. Now, as we prayed together, Karen grappled with accepting God's authority when it didn't seem to fit with what she wanted.

She prayed, "Lord, what You say in Your Word sometimes doesn't seem right to me. I don't see how it can *work*. . . . And at times I just don't like what You tell me! I wonder then, Do you really know what's best for me? . . . Should I obey You?"

*   *   *   *

Doesn't this sound a great deal like the last verse in the Book of Judges, "Every man did what was right in his own eyes" (Judges 21:25 RSV)?

In 1 Samuel 2 and 3 great emphasis is placed on the issue of authority, and in particular respect for the Lord and His ways. There is a striking contrast here between the children of two families: Eli, the high priest's family and Samuel's family. This contrast also has strong overtones for today's society, where once again authority is a primary issue.

During the time Eli's sons were growing up, they had been increasingly influenced by the ungodly societies around them. In order to better understand the actions of Hophni and Phinehas, let's look at these influences.

Cultural Insights

Canaanite Religion: When the children of Israel came into the Promised Land, God commanded them to drive out the people who lived there: the Canaanites. God did not want their heathen religious practices influencing the lives of His people.

The Canaanites believed in more than seventy gods, and they "accepted" anything one chose to believe. Thus, they were very "accepting" toward Israel's God, Yahweh, wanting to add Him to their pantheon, or group, of gods.

The key to the Canaanite religion is a mythological cycle involving four gods. This cycle seemed to explain the changing of the seasons to these agricultural people.

The Canaanite religious cycle went like this: In the spring the land became fertile and productive because Baal (god of rain and fertility) defeated Mot (god of death) or Yam (god of the Salt Sea). The victorious Baal was then crowned king, and every year a holy marriage took place between Baal and Anat (goddess of sex and war). When Baal and Anat began liv-

*Canaanite
Religion:*

ing together, the earth became fertile in every way—plants, animals, and humans all multiplied.

Later, in the summer, Mot or Yam defeated Baal and the land grew dry and parched. In the late fall and winter months, Anat came and revived Baal, who in turn defeated Mot, bringing the rains of springtime. Baal and Anat would then marry, and so the cycle continued.

The practical outworking of this religious cycle in the lives of the Canaanites was devastating, for they believed that their actions affected the gods. Wanting to "encourage" the gods, they placed prostitutes, both male and female, in the temple. Their sexual relations with each other or with visitors were a part of the "worship" service. Their actions were to serve as a model for Baal and Anat, the makers of new life.

The Canaanites thought they could appease and bribe the gods by sacrificing children and young virgins, and by worshiping snakes and the dead. They tried to manipulate and thus control their gods. Their religious system was abhorrent to the living God.

God was jealous for His people. "You shall not bow down to them or worship them; for I, the LORD your God, am a jealous God" (Deut. 5:9). He wanted His people to remain faithful, but He feared they would allow, then accept, then settle down with, and finally *practice* the Canaanite religion. And this is exactly what happened!

High Priest: Head of the religious hierarchy of Israel. As
                 the chief representative of the people before
                 God, he presided over issues of the law and
                 the worship services.

Lamp   The seven-branched candlestick that provided
of God: the light for the Holy Place in the temple.

Discovery 1 / The Priest's Family / (2:12–17, 22)

1. With a graphic description, God begins His commentary
   on the family that led the nation of Israel at the time of
   Samuel's birth.

   In v. 12 how does God characterize the sons of Eli?

   _____

   _____

   _____

   List the specific offenses committed by Eli's sons. (Leviti-
   cus 3:3–5 states more fully God's sacrificial law.) What
   did the disobedience of Eli's sons show they thought of
   God and His ways?

   _____

   _____

   _____

   In light of your study to this point, who or what had Eli's
   sons chosen to follow? Why would it have been impossible for them to truly lead the people in worshiping God?

   _____

   _____

   _____

2. According to v. 17, what did the actions of Eli's sons reveal about their heart attitude toward God and His ways?

_____

In some areas could God conclude this from your actions? Explain. Would this be His summary of the behavior of your children? What are you doing about this?

_____

_____

_____

3. In light of the cultural insights given at the beginning of this lesson, were the actions of Eli's sons (v. 22) "culturally" acceptable? Explain.

_____

_____

Read Deuteronomy 5:7, 9. In light of this and what you've learned about the Canaanite religion, why were the actions of Eli's sons not acceptable to God?

_____

_____

List actions that today's society accepts, but which God, in His Word, says are not acceptable. Do you take part in any of these activities? If so, what does your participation say about your heart attitude toward God's Word?

_____

_____

_____

_____

Discovery 2 / A Wise Mother / (2:18–21)

4. In the midst of the commentary on Eli's family, what contrasting picture is drawn in vv. 18–21?

   _____

   What might Hannah's actions have revealed to Samuel about her heart attitude toward God and His ways?

   _____

5. With what particular blessing did God respond to Hannah's heart after God? (vv. 20–21).

   _____

   In what way are vv. 20–21 an illustration of the promises found in Psalm 37:4–6 and Psalm 84:11?

   _____

   Do you think Samuel would have noticed the outworking of God's blessing in his mother's life? Support your answer.

   _____

   Do you think your children see the outworking of God's blessing in your life? Specifically how?

   _____

Discovery 3 / A Foolish Father / (2:22–36)

6. To counteract the influence of pagan culture, what instruction was Eli to give his sons according to Deuteronomy 6:4–9? Where was this to take place?

   _____

   _____

   _____

Though chapters 1 and 2 show Eli as a somewhat sincere priest, what habitual sin is pointed out in 2:29 and 3:13?

_____

7. What verb is repeated three times in vv. 22–24? What appears to be the greatest motivation for Eli rebuking his sons?

_____

_____

How did Eli's sons respond to their father's authority? Support your answer from the insights found in vv. 22–25.

_____

_____

In light of vv. 27–29, where might Eli's sons first have learned how to fulfill their selfish desires?

_____

_____

8. State the consequences God said would result from the sin of Eli and his sons (2:30–36).

_____

_____

What warning might the story of Eli and his sons be for parents today? In light of the tragic circumstances of 2:27–29 and 3:13, what trait seems crucial to teach to our children? (See also Proverbs 1:7.)

_____

_____

_____

9. Summarize chapter 2 by stating the contrasts in the following sets of verses:

   11 and 12 _____

   17 and 18 _____

   25 and 26 _____

Discovery 4 / God Calls Samuel / (3:1–18)

10. What significant character trait does Samuel demonstrate in vv. 1–9?

   _____

   How did Samuel show respect for Eli?

   _____

11. Read vv. 10–14. What did Samuel do when he finally realized that God was calling him? Then, what did God do?

   _____

   _____

12. According to v. 15, how did Samuel feel about telling Eli the content of his vision? Why might he have felt this way?

   _____

   _____

   However difficult it may have been, to what degree was Samuel obedient to the one in authority over him? (vv. 16–18).

   _____

   _____

13. What type of response did Samuel's first declaration of God's Word receive? What did Eli's reaction indicate he knew about God?

_____

_____

Discovery 5 / A Biblical Principle Stands / (2:30; 3:19–21)

14. In your own words, write the important principle God set forth in 1 Samuel 2:30.

_____

15. What words would you use to describe the atmosphere that surrounded Samuel as he grew up?

_____

Does it appear Samuel was corrupted by the influences around him? Explain, supporting your answer with verses from chapter 2. How might this be an encouragement to you if your child is in a difficult home, school, neighborhood, or work environment?

_____

_____

_____

16. What four ways, found in 3:19–21, did Samuel's honoring the Lord through obedience result in God's blessing upon Samuel or upon others?

_____

_____

_____

_____

What personal challenge have you discovered in this section?

_____

*   *   *   *

Key Principles from Lesson 3

1. A healthy concept of the God-given place of authority is necessary for spiritual maturity. If we do not trust and obey authorities, we will not grow properly. (2:1–3:18)
2. We must decide who will be our ultimate authority—God or self.
3. God will judge ungodly religious leaders. (2:17; 3:11–14).
4. Continuing disrespect for God and His ways brings discipline and judgment. (2:17, 27–34)
5. Faithfulness in speaking God's Word shows that we are fit to be His voices in the world. Samuel's mother had been faithful to a difficult promise (3:15–18); and in Samuel's first real test, we see the effect of this modeling on him. Despite being afraid, he faithfully spoke the word of the Lord.
6. If we honor God, He will honor us; and if we despise Him, we will be lightly esteemed. We despise God by choosing our way over His. His Word and His spokesmen in the world make His way clear (2:30).

4

"BUT I'VE GOT PROBLEMS!"

1 Samuel 4–7

It was Tuesday morning, and our neighborhood prayer group was meeting at our house. That morning the theme of our prayers seemed to be, "Lord, deliver me!"

One person prayed, "Lord, my problem is *him*. Straighten him out and I'll be able to follow your ways!"

Another said, "Lord take *her* out of my life!"

And another prayed, "Lord, my problem is *them*. They don't seem to care. I'd be faithful if they would just care!"

*   *   *   *

So often we look at what "seems" to be the major problem in our life and think, *If this were just taken care of, all would be well.*

This is exactly what the Israelites thought as they faced the Philistines. "Help! We're in trouble!" From the human perspective their problem *was* imposing! The Israelites saw the Philistines and all their weapons and it was hard to think of anything else. However, a closer look at the passage helps us realize that the Israelites' real problem was not the Philistines! They were very close to recognizing the real issue after their first defeat, and they were close to asking the right questions, but they were not listening for God's answers.

Often we, too, want God's deliverance but not His ways.

Cultural Insights

Samuel:
With great discernment, Samuel looked at the tremendous needs of his nation, a people who wanted God's blessing but not His ways. Through Moses, God had given Israel His principles of living. However, the people had turned away from these principles and regressed to having the morals of barbarians. Now, at Israel's lowest point, when everything seemed hopeless, Samuel was used to stop the nation's decay and preserve the people as a nation.

In chapters 4–7 Samuel is busy putting a country together. Under the guidance of the Holy Spirit, he began restoring the moral and religious life of the people. He became the focal point of Israel's religious and political life, voluntarily traveling in a circuit of the country each year and administering Israel's spiritual and political affairs. Samuel thus became the link between two periods of Israel's history, the period of the judges and that of the monarchy.

Prophet:
The prophetic office began when God confirmed Samuel as a prophet. Although the word had been used to describe others before Samuel, the office had never before been or-

ganized. Samuel was very likely the founder of the important schools of the prophets mentioned in 1 Samuel 10:11. From Samuel's time on, the prophets sought to cultivate the spiritual life of the nation. They were the means through which God's will was made known to the king and the people.

The Ark: The symbol of God's holy presence. Israel's neighboring nations looked upon the ark as the god of Israel (4:6–7). The ark was a chest made of a strong wood that grew in the desert, acacia wood. This frame was overlaid with pure gold.

On top of the chest were representations of two cherubim, made of gold, with outstretched wings. They guarded the holiness of the mercy seat. The two tablets of stone, upon which the Ten Commandments were written, were kept in the ark. (The Commandments stated the terms of God's covenant with His people.) ? *Obedience*

Astaroth: The Philistines' popular goddess of sex and pleasure.

Dagon: One of the major Philistine gods.

Discovery 1 / A Desperate Problem / (Chapter 4)

Commit your study time to the Lord. Ask Him to open your eyes to see principles from this narrative that relate to your own life circumstances. Then act on what you discover.

1. Explain what happened to the Israelites in the battle against the Philistines. (vv. 1–2)

_____

_____

2. In light of this, what important question did the leaders of the Israelites ask? Why might this have been a wise question? What do their actions tell us about what they thought the answer was?

_____

_____

_____

3. By bringing the ark to the battlefield, what do you think Israel was attempting to do? Though Samuel was known throughout the land as a prophet (3:19–4:1), is there any indication that Israel sought his counsel? What does this say?

_____

_____

4. State the emotional response of Israel when the ark arrived at the scene of battle. (v. 5)

_____

What was the response of the enemy and why? (vv. 6–8)

_____

_____

5. What effect did the presence of the ark have upon the battle? Why?

_____

_____

_____

That day how do you think Israel's God "looked" to those who did not know Him?

_____

_____

6. What specific fulfillment of prophecy (2:30–36) was seen in the events of 4:10–22? How would God have "looked" to one who remembered and had respect for God's Word concerning this fateful day?

_____

_____

7. How does the dying wife of the priest Phinehas sum up the tragedy? (vv. 21–22)

_____

_____

Read Psalm 78:56–61 and Jeremiah 7:12–14, 23, 24. How does God sum up His reasons for the tragedy? What phrase in Psalm 78:61 shows how the Philistines were able to capture the ark?

_____

_____

_____

Though Israel saw her problem as being the Philistines, what was her real problem? As you have studied this lesson, has any new light been shed on your problems? If so, what?

_____

_____

_____

What do you learn about God through this passage that would affect your life as a single woman, wife, or mother? In what way or ways?

_____

_____

Challenge Question: Suddenly, literally within hours, the leadership of the country rested on the shoulders of the young man Samuel. How had God prepared Samuel for this important day in his life?

_____

_____

_____

Discovery 2 / Unbelievers See God's Character / (Chapter 5)

8. Refer to the map on page 16 to find Aphek, Ashdod, Gath, and Ekron.

   What attitude did the Philistines display as they placed the ark of the covenant alongside their god, Dagon? (vv. 1–2) List ways this same attitude is displayed today.

   _____

   _____

9. In God's perfect time, He showed Himself as God to the Philistines. State the specific ways in which God demonstrated His power to:

   Those in Ashdod. (vv. 1–7)

   _____

   Those in Gath. (vv. 8–9)

   _____

Those in Ekron. (vv. 10–12)

What was the continual result of the ark being treated and used in the wrong way?

Discovery 3 / The Philistines Respond to God / (6:1–12)

10. Read 6:1–12. What consciousness did the ark of the Lord bring to the Philistines? (vv. 2–3)

In order to show them that He was God, what three Philistine possessions did God attack? (v. 5) How might this discipline have humbled the Philistines?

11. To free themselves from God's hand of judgment, what specific action did the Philistine priests tell their people to take? (vv. 5–8)

12. What "impossible" test did the Philistine priests set up to "check out" God? (vv. 7–12) According to v. 9, who or what was responsible for circumstances if not God?

In what way does the result of the test demonstrate God's power and sovereign control over His creation? How might this test and its results encourage you this week?

_____

_____

_____

What have you learned about God from Discoveries 2 and 3? Describe a present-day situation in which God has shown His power and character to mockers.

_____

_____

_____

Discovery 4 / An Old Lesson Relearned / (6:13–21)

13. Read vv. 13–21, along with Numbers 4:5, 15, 20. What lesson, just learned by the Philistines, had the Israelites forgotten?

_____

_____

Read Exodus 19:9–19; 20:18–23. In light of these verses, why do you think God was particularly firm in his dealings with the men of Beth Shemesh?

_____

_____

How might disrespect for God and His ways be shown in: your home, your community, your country, the world? (Note: Carelessness or casualness can be a sign of disrespect.)

_____

_____

_____

Discovery 5 / Israel Responds to God / (Chapter 7)

14. How many years did God's people wait to hear Him speak? (v. 2)

_____

_____

What four conditions did God give His people through His spokesman, Samuel? If the conditions were met, what was the promised result?

_____

_____

_____

_____

_____

Even before Samuel spoke what should Israel have understood about returning to the Lord? (See Exodus 20: 1–5, 23; Deuteronomy 4:39–40; 8:19–20; 30:15–20.)

_____

_____

As you compared Samuel's message with these earlier directives, what lessons did you learn for your own life?

_____

_____

_____

15. What specific actions accompanied Israel's heart attitude of genuine repentance? (vv. 4–6)

_____

_____

_____

What, then, does this suggest is involved in repentance?

_____

16. When the people were suddenly confronted with their old "problem" (v. 7), how did they respond emotionally?

_____

Despite their feelings, what did the people *do* about the problem? (vv. 8–9, 11) (Refer also to vv. 3–6.)

_____

_____

What corresponding principle might you apply when one of your "old problems" suddenly reappears?

_____

17. When the Israelites obeyed God, how did He respond? (vv. 3–14)

_____

Can you give an example of a time you obeyed God's directions and He brought deliverance?

_____

18. In your opinion, why did Samuel set up a monument? (vv. 11–12)

_____

When God brings victory to you or your family, how might a commemorative "stone" serve the same purpose as Samuel's? Name a specific way you might follow Samuel's example.

_____

_____

* * * *

Key Principles from Lesson 4

1. By bringing a problem into your life, God may disclose to you hidden sins and sinful attitudes of the heart. (4:2–23)
2. The object of our faith must be God, not crosses, church buildings, religious shrines, worship services, etc.
3. God is faithful in performing His Word. (4:10–11, 16–22 with 2:31–36)
4. This world's gods are powerless before God Almighty. (Chapters 5 and 6)
5. Respect and honor should be given to God's ways. Disrespect, including casualness concerning the Spirit of God, the Scriptures, and spiritual gifts, may bring discipline. (6:19–21)
6. Genuine repentance includes turning away from the sin or removing the temptation. Saying "I am sorry," is not enough. Real repentance leads to constructive action. (7:3–6)
7. Deliverance will follow genuine repentance. (7:3–4)
8. Following God's instructions shows reverence for God and demonstrates that He is the authority in our lives (7:3–13)
9. It is helpful to remember God's victories in a visual way. (7:12)

5

"I HAVE NEEDS YOU KNOW!"

1 Samuel 8–10

Mary Lou went from Bible conference to Bible study to family seminar, never taking time to reflect on all the material filling up her notebook, never acting on what she was learning.

She would look at others whose lives where changing, and she wanted her life to change too. But rather than applying what she was learning to her own life, she complained continually. For example, she would pray:

"Lord, I'm miserable and it's because I don't have a husband." Unfortunately, her needs changed frequently: a husband, a house, a baby, a new sofa, a car, a job, success!

In each case, she would say, "Lord, my life will be different when I have this. I'll have good attitudes then. I'll be happy!"

To those who warned her that there are consequences to relying on *things*, she would say, "Right now I don't care about the consequences. Anything's better than the way things are going. I know what I need, and I want it!"

*　　*　　*　　*

What we think our needs are and what our *real* needs are may be two very different things. Our lesson will deal with this issue as well as illustrate that troubles increase when we try to meet our needs other than in God's way.

In 1 Samuel 7 we saw peace and order come to Israel when she carefully followed God's instructions. In time, however, she once again became lax about the things of God and became increasingly involved with foreign gods. And once again discipline came by way of attacks by other nations. Then, in 1 Samuel 8, the pivotal chapter of this book of the Bible, Israel cries out for a king.

It was also at this time that Samuel entered perhaps the most difficult years of his life. Yet, true to his calling, he is faithful as the leader of the nation as well as an obedient servant of God. Thus Samuel is used by God to establish the new period of the kings. The period of the judges ends and a new era begins.

Cultural Insights

Kingship: In the ancient Near East, the first-born son was normally the successor to the throne. However, Israel had never had a king. Her first king was chosen by God, anointed by the prophet, and revealed to the people by God's leading of the prophet.

Benjamin: The nation of Israel was divided into twelve tribes. Benjamin, one of the smaller tribes, may not have seemed as important as the others. Judges 20 says this tribe was almost wiped out by the other eleven tribes because of its immoral conduct. Saul, the first king of Israel, was a Benjamite.

Discovery 1 / The Request / (8:1–10, 20)

The psalmist prayed, "Direct my footsteps according to your Word" (119:133). Right now, ask the Lord to do the same for you.

1. List three ways Samuel's sons broke the command of God as stated in Deuteronomy 16:18–20. (vv. 1–3)

   _____

   _____

   _____

2. In vv. 4–5, 20, what reasons did the people give for "needing" an earthly king?

   _____

   Does it seem the sin of Samuel's sons was the real reason the children of Israel wanted a king? Explain.

   _____

   What did God see as the true issue behind the request? (vv. 7–8)

   _____

3. Contrast the people's request in 7:7–8 with that in 8:20. How had their view of God changed? (See 1 Chronicles 29:11 for further insight.)

   _____

   _____

   Can you describe a time your requests (or someone else's) demonstrated a similar contrast?

   _____

   _____

4. What emotional effect did their request have upon Samuel? (vv. 6–7) What might have been the cause(s) of such a reaction?

_____

_____

_____

In v. 6 what did Samuel do about the people's request and his own reaction to it? How can Samuel's action be a model for our response to the demands of others?

_____

_____

_____

In your own words state the Lord's counsel to Samuel found in vv. 7–9.

_____

How did the Lord comfort Samuel? (vv. 7–8)

_____

5. After bringing his dilemma to the Lord and listening to God's answer, what did Samuel do in v. 10?

_____

Discovery 2 / The Consequences / (8:11–22)

6. In vv. 11–17 God foretells the consequences of the people getting what they want. List these.

_____

_____

_____

How does God say the people will view their request *after* they experience the consequences? (v. 18)

_____

Although God knew the future, He did not have to warn His people. What does His warning them say about his character and concern?

_____

7. What effect did God's warning have upon the people? Be specific in your answer. (vv. 19–20)

_____

Can you describe a time you responded in a similar manner?

_____

8. In chapter 8 what have you learned about God that could make a difference in your life as a woman, wife, or mother? Be specific, citing the verse that supports your answer.

_____

How would the truths you've learned about God in this lesson affect your requests to Him?

_____

Discovery 3 / The People Wait—God Acts / (9:1–18)

9. Saul's search mission (vv. 3–18) must have been frustrating. In what verse, and in what ways, is the one responsible for Saul's circumstances revealed?

_____

_____

10. What role does a prophet play in the selection of a king? (See 1 Samuel 9:27–10:1; 16:1–13; 1 Kings 1:32–35.) In what ways did God prepare Samuel for his involvement in selecting the king? (8:22; 9:14–18) What did Samuel "do" to find the chosen king?

_____

_____

_____

List at least three principles concerning God or His ways that you have discovered in answering the preceding question; think of a specific way you could apply this principle to your life as a single woman, a wife, or a mother.

1. _____

_____

2. _____

_____

3. _____

_____

Discovery 4 / Samuel Prepares Saul / (9:19–27)

11. When Saul asked a stranger for the address of the prophet's house, what startling answer did he receive? (vv. 19–20) What does Saul's response indicate about his character? (v. 21)

_____

_____

_____

List at least three specific things Samuel did to help prepare and encourage the young man, Saul, who was overwhelmed with Samuel's words (vv. 21–27)

_____

_____

_____

Discovery 5 / Samuel Anoints Saul as King / (Chapter 10)

12. Despite his feelings concerning the kingship (8:6, 19–22), what is Samuel faithful to do in 10:1? (See also 8:22.)

_____

What is the inheritance spoken of in Deuteronomy 32:9 and Psalm 78:71?

_____

What, then, is taking place in 1 Samuel 10:1?

_____

13. What character trait does Saul demonstrate in 9:21 and 10:14–16, 20–22, as well as in Samuel's commentary on this time in 15:17?

_____

14. What more did God do to encourage the heart of Saul? How does this show God's sovereignty? What happened to Saul's heart perspective? (v.9) How would this have prepared Saul for leadership?

_____

_____

_____

_____

15. Before Saul was declared king, what did God again emphasize to the people of Israel? (vv. 18–19)

    _____

    _____

16. When Saul is introduced, what about him is noted? (vv. 23–24) Do you think this very characteristic might have encouraged the people to view him as a king? Why?

    _____

    _____

17. According to Deuteronomy 17:14–20, what were to be the rules of the new kingdom?

    _____

    _____

    What would our government be like if these rules were heeded today? Explain.

    _____

    _____

18. After being hailed king, what immediate problem did Saul face? What was his response? (v. 27) What type of person do you see him as? Support your answer with Scripture.

    _____

    _____

    _____

    _____

    _____

    *   *   *   *

Key Principles from Lesson 5

1. We will discover the following key principles as we continue our study of 1 Samuel. *Troubles increase when we choose the seemingly easier, more attractive human way in place of God and His way as revealed in His Word.* To wait, trusting in God alone, may seem hard, but it is best! (8:5, 9, 19, 20)

2. We should not use the faults of those in leadership positions as excuses for our own selfish desires. (8:4–5)

3. Difficult situations should be taken to the Lord. (8:6, 21)

4. Through His Word, God lovingly and faithfully warns of the consequences of not following His way. We are foolish not to give heed. (8:11–17)

5. Many people feel they are an exception to God's rule. (8:19–20)

6. God is sovereign. (9:1–18; 10:2–13, 20–21)

6

"WHAT DO I DO NOW THAT I'VE SINNED?"

1 Samuel 11–12

I was writing the title for this lesson when the phone rang.

"What do you do when you've sinned, and you really want to stop the train you're on?" the young mother on the other end soon asked. "I've been so selfish, trying to get what *I* want. And my actions have really hurt my family. I knew I was sinning, but I turned to food instead of to God. Now everything's a mess.

"I know I've been wrong. What do I do now?"

*   *   *   *

After we realize that we've sinned, we, too, ask the question, "What do I do now?" In this lesson God answers this very practical question through His spokesman Samuel.

Cultural Insights

Saul's Task: At the time of Saul's inauguration, Israel's twelve tribes were like separate entities, harboring differences and jealousies among themselves. The unifying influence of worshiping at a central sanctuary had been lost with the destruction of Shiloh after the battle of Aphek (1 Sam. 4). King Saul's first job was to unify these tribes into a real nation. Samuel had lain a firm groundwork for this unity through his circuit ministry, which restored morale and renewed the people's faith in God.

The people of Israel were hardly ready for a complex government with rigid controls. Although unity was the goal, the old tribal borders were still observed. The manner in which Saul began his rule showed insight and good judgment, for the new central form of government had to be accepted gradually and not forced on the people overnight.

During the period of the judges, Palestine had been continually disturbed by many outside nations; the twelve tribes had been forced to concentrate on survival. However, for the major portion of the rule of Israel's first three kings, she was not bothered by any major international power (e.g., Egypt). So the nation was able to mature, and expand its boundaries.

Saul's Style: Saul set up the capital in his hometown of Gibeah. The palace was of simple design. In fact, excavators have termed it "more like a dungeon than a royal residence, in comparison with the Canaanite masonry with which Solomon graced Jerusalem."

The royal court was not elaborate either. Scripture names only one officer of Saul's court—Abner, captain of the army as well as Saul's cousin (1 Sam. 20:24–27).

The well-known archaeologist, W. F. Albright, said: "Saul was only a rustic chieftan as far as the amenities of life were concerned." But this observation could also be applied to Israel's culture as a whole; she was rustic and poor until the reigns of David and Solomon.

Ammonites: A people related to Israel through Abraham's nephew, Lot (Gen. 19:38). Their lifestyle was nomadic, and they were savage in character (Amos 1:13). Probably some time before Israel had begged for a human king, the king of the Ammonites, Nahash, had begun penetrating Israel's fertile and lush valley of Jabesh-gilead, destroying its barley fields, olive plantations, and small villages. The capital city of the Gilead area was Jabesh-gilead (the city besieged in 1 Sam. 11), located on top of an isolated hill and overlooking the southern end of the valley.

Discovery 1 / A Desperate Problem / (11:1–3)

"Your Word is a lamp to my feet, a light for my path" (Ps. 119:105).

Stop now and ask the Lord to make this verse real for you as you study.

Note: As you study, find on your map the locations mentioned in the Scriptures. (See p. 16.)

1. What did the people of Jabesh-gilead do when the Ammonites besieged their city? (v. 1)

_____

In the panic of the moment, have you ever made similar decisions? Give a specific example.

_____

2. State King Nahash's insolent reply to the city's appeal. (v. 2)

_____

What do you think the phrase "and so bring disgrace on all Israel" means? (For further insight read 1 Samuel 7:26 and Psalm 44:13.)

_____

3. What did the elders of Jabesh ask of Nahash? (v. 3)

_____

Why might Nahash have consented to their request?

_____

Discovery 2 / Response! / (11:4–10)

4. What did the people of Gibeah _do_ when they heard the news of the siege? (v. 4) What might have been the cause of such a response? Would this type of response have helped the people of Jabesh?

_____

_____

_____

_____

_____

5. In contrast, how did Saul react to the news? (vv. 5–7)

_____

According to vv. 6–7, what made the difference between the two responses?

_____

Discovery 3 / Saul Is King! / (11:11–15)

6. In contrast to the battle at Aphek (chapter 4), what key man supported and stood with Saul as the nation of Israel was called to battle at Jabesh-gilead? (vv. 7, 14)

_____

What do you think this meant? (Let 1 Samuel 3:19–21; 7:7–9 help you answer.)

_____

7. Describe the response of the whole nation as they heard Saul's challenge. (vv. 7–10)

_____

What phrase indicates the source of this response?

_____

8. How did the people feel about Saul at the end of the battle? (vv. 12, 15)

_____

9. How did Saul describe the victory at Jabesh? (v. 13) What does this statement reveal about him at this time?

_____

_____

_____

In v. 15 what are the results of Saul and the people following God's ways?

_____

_____

List at least two principles for living that you discovered in vv. 11–15. Choose one of these principles and describe a specific situation in which the principle may be helpful to you this week.

_____

_____

_____

_____

Discovery 4 / Faithful Samuel Speaks Out / (12:1–18)

10. List the specific leadership qualifications that gave Samuel the respect of the people due God's spokesman. (vv. 1–5)

_____

_____

_____

What important lessons concerning godly leadership may be gleaned from vv. 1–5? First Timothy 3:1–12 and Titus 1:7–9 also describe the characteristics religious leaders are to have. Compare these three Scriptures.

_____

_____

_____

_____

This passage encourages mothers or teachers to build up what traits in their children? Give a specific illustration of how this might be accomplished.

_____

11. List the faithful works of the real King of Israel, as Samuel describes them in vv. 8–13. In a second list, record the reaction of God's people. What personal challenge does this contrast bring to light?

    God's Works:

    _____

    _____

    Israel's Reaction:

    _____

    _____

    Personal Challenge:

    _____

    _____

12. What does v. 12 suggest as the real motive behind the people's request for an earthly king?

    _____

    What sin had the people of God committed? (v. 12) How might we be guilty of the same sin?

    _____

    _____

13. Picking up the pieces: Despite having an earthly king, who were the people to serve? (vv. 14–15)

    _____

List at least four specific ways God's children are to serve their heavenly King. List a specific way you can carry out these four commands. (v. 14) (Consider: specifics as a single woman, wife, mother, church member, citizen.)

1. _____

_____

2. _____

_____

3. _____

_____

4. _____

_____

What would happen to the people if they were unfaithful? (v. 15)

_____

14. How did God symbolically prove the truth of Samuel's speech? (vv. 17–18)

_____

_____

What does this reveal about God?

_____

Discovery 5 / God Supports His Spokesman / (12:19–25)

15. What effect did Samuel's words, emphasized by God's demonstration, have upon the people? (vv. 18–19)

_____

_____

What do you think the people finally realized?

_____

_____

16. In light of their response, how does Samuel encourage the people in vv. 20–21?

    _____

    _____

    What is the basis for his encouragement? (v. 22)

    _____

    _____

    Why must the people *not* lose their focus on God? What will happen if they do? (v. 21)

    _____

    _____

17. In vv. 23–24 what did God's faithful spokesman promise to do for the people, even though they had, in part, rejected him?

    _____

    Search your own heart. Is there someone you are praying for despite his or her unfaithfulness or rejection?

    _____

18. In your own words, write Samuel's final challenge (vv. 24–25) as if it were written to you.

    _____

    _____

*   *   *   *

Key Principles from Lesson 6

1. Our response to others' needs may be merely emotional or that of spirit-directed action. (12:1–7)

2. Rebellious people ask for something more than God Himself. (12:12)

3. After we have matured enough to realize that we have been wrong, we may wonder, "What do I do now?" God's answer, through Samuel, is fourfold: (1) fear or reverence the Lord; (2) serve Him; (3) obey His voice; (4) rebel not against His commands. You will know that you are following the Lord if you are heeding these four directives. (12:14)

4. Turning from the Lord and toward useless things which have no power to deliver us is futile. (12:21)

5. Despite the way we are treated by those we serve, we are never to stop praying for them and instructing them in the good and right way. (12:23)

6. If we continue to rebel against a command of God, the hand of God will discipline us, so that we might return to His ways.

7

"WHY OBEDIENCE?"

1 Samuel 13–15

Carrie was great with words.

"I'm going to follow what God says . . ." she would say. "I'm going to listen, and then obey Him."

She seemed very sincere. Many were fooled; perhaps she even fooled herself. But as one got to know Carrie, a pattern could be seen in her life: her actions and her words did not line up. When confronted she would make herself appear innocent and others guilty.

Then she would say, "Yes, I know what I said about obeying God. And I would, if it weren't for people doing things that keep me from it."

*   *   *   *

Obedience to His ways is at the very center of what God wants for His children. He knows that only then will it "go well with them and their children forever" (Deut. 5:29).

Obedience is also at the heart of how to love God. Jesus

said, "If you love me, you will obey what I command" (John 14:15).

In this lesson we will see what happens when a man loves God and obeys Him, as well as what happens when one compromises God's Word.

Cultural Insights

Amalekites: Descendants of Esau (Gen. 36:12). Having attacked the Israelites in the Sinai during their exodus from Egypt, they remained Israel's constant and cruel enemies.

Philistine Iron Smiths: The Philistines were the first in Palestine to learn the secret of iron smelting. Holding the secrets to this craft, they were able to control the use of iron weapons, which were superior to the bronze weapons used by other nations of Palestine.

Discovery 1 / Trouble Brews / (13:1–7)

1. How old was Saul when he became king and how long did he rule? With the great victory at Jabesh-gilead behind him, Saul and his son Jonathan prepare to free Israel from subjection to the Philistines; at first it goes well. How does Saul attempt to stir up a unified army? (vv. 1–4)

   _____

   _____

2. When the new army of Israel arrived, what great problem faced them? Be specific. (vv. 5–6)

   _____

   _____

What a test for Saul! Put yourself in his place. What reactions might you have had?

_____

_____

Why was the routing of the Philistines so important? Why couldn't they just peacefully coexist in the same land? (See Deut. 6:13–15; 12:29–31; 1 Sam. 7:3 for further insight.)

_____

_____

3. List the various ways the children of Israel responded to their problem. (vv. 6–7)

_____

_____

Read God's Word to His children recorded in Deuteronomy 7:17–21. In the emotion of the moment, what was Saul's army forgetting?

_____

_____

Do you find your response to a current problem similar to Israel's? In light of Deuteronomy 7:17–21, Philippians 4:6–7 and Hebrews 12:2 how are we to face problems? What has God promised us if we follow His instructions?

_____

_____

_____

_____

Discovery 2 / Saul Reacts / (13:5–23)

4. As the leader of his army, what pressures did Saul face?
   (vv. 5–8)

   _____

   _____

   Through His spokesman Samuel, God had given Saul
   specific instructions concerning this crisis. What were
   these instructions, found in 10:8? What did God promise
   in return for obedience?

   _____

   _____

   _____

5. Under pressure, what decision did King Saul make? (v. 9)

   _____

   Immediately after Saul carried out his decision, what
   happened? (v. 10)

   _____

   "What have you done?" Samuel asked Saul. After reading vv. 11–13, what do you think Saul's sin was? (See
   also 15:22–23.)

   _____

   Have you ever felt God moved too slowly and that
   "something" had to be done? Describe a situation where
   you took things into your own hands.

   _____

   _____

   _____

Upon what was Saul focusing as he faced his responsibility and God's commands concerning it? (vv. 11–12)

Below are listed four areas of responsibility. The Bible gives commands concerning these. Evaluate each responsibility that pertains to you by considering if your response is similar to Saul's.

(1) your responsibilities to your husband/wife (Eph. 5:33)
(2) to your children (Prov. 22:6)
(3) to your friends (John 13:34–35)
(4) for another ministry or calling God has given you (1 Peter 4:11)

6. What was the result of Saul's sin? (vv. 13–15)

In light of what Saul has done, what do you think the key phrase *"a man after God's own heart"* means? Personalize your answer; what does it mean for you to be after His own heart?

According to 2 Chronicles 16:9, what will God *do* for one who has a fully committed heart?

---

7. Read vv. 16–23. In any battle, what distinct disadvantage did Israel have and why? First Samuel has demonstrated that Israel's God is in control of all things. Who must have allowed this "disadvantage" to exist? How and why might God allow you to fight your battles while seemingly disadvantaged?

_____

_____

_____

_____

_____

Discovery 3 / Jonathan Reacts / (14:1–23)

8. Contrast Jonathan's approach to the Philistine problem with Saul's approach as found in 13:8–12. (vv. 1–14)

_____

_____

_____

What would you say Jonathan knows about God? How does he demonstrate this knowledge? (Support your answer by citing the proper verse.)

_____

_____

_____

List three principles seen in Jonathan's approach to the problem facing his nation that could be applied to a situation you are currently facing.

_____

_____

_____

9. What effect did the faith of Jonathan and his armor bearer have upon the people? (vv. 16, 20–22)

_____

10. What do Exodus 14:30 and 2 Chronicles 32:20–22 have in common with the testimony of v. 23?

_____

_____

Write your own statement describing a deliverance the Lord has given you.

_____

_____

_____

Discovery 4 / A Rash Statement Causes Sin / (14:24–52)

11. What might have been Saul's motives for his command in vv. 24–26? What did he not take into account? (v. 23)

_____

_____

What does it appear God had provided for His weary army?

_____

_____

12. How might Saul's command have been detrimental to Israel's cause? (v. 30)

_____

_____

Can you identify a rash command of yours that caused hardship for others?

_____

_____

What specific command of God (Gen. 9:4; Lev. 17: 10–14) did the hungry soldiers break? What did Saul do about it? (vv. 31–35)

_____

_____

In vv. 43, 45, how did God save Jonathan?

_____

_____

13. How was Saul's leadership undermined by the conversation that took place in vv. 44–45?

_____

_____

What principles discovered in vv. 24–45 can be applied by mothers or women in other roles of authority?

_____

_____

Discovery 5 / Saul's View of God's Commands / (Chapter 15)

14. What was God's specific command to King Saul in vv. 1–3? In light of Exodus 17:8–16 what important mission was Saul to carry out?

_____

_____

Did Saul carry out God's command? Explain. How did Saul's actions in vv. 4–9, 12–13 reveal his attitudes concerning God?

_____

_____

15. How did Saul respond when confronted by Samuel? (vv. 13–15, 20–21) What kind of a leader does this imply he was? Compare Saul's response with Adam's in Genesis 3:6–12.

    _____

    _____

    How did Samuel feel about the Lord's message to him? (vv. 10–12, 35) What did Samuel do about his emotions?

    _____

    _____

    What kind of a leader does this suggest Samuel was?

    _____

    _____

16. Read vv. 16–31. What did Samuel tell Saul he had done wrong? What was Saul's initial response? (vv. 17–21)

    _____

    _____

    According to vv. 22–23, what important truth about God had Saul missed?

    _____

    _____

    Whom had Saul feared? To whose voice had he listened? (v. 24)

    _____

    _____

    _____

Do you think Saul was genuinely repentant? Give verses to support your opinion.

_____

_____

Search your own heart. Have you rejected some aspect of the Word of the Lord? In what area? To whose voice have you been listening? Now that you are aware of your sin, what should you do about it?

_____

_____

_____

_____

Challenge Question: In light of v. 29, what do you think God meant when He said that He regretted having made Saul king over Israel? (v. 35)

_____

_____

*   *   *   *

Key Principles from Lesson 7

1. In a crisis, obeying God's directives is always the safest path for us to follow. (13:13)
2. A heart that does not try to compromise God's command is a heart that is His. A heart that desires to follow the Lord and obey His command is a heart after His heart. (15:20)
3. God's delight is in our obeying Him, not in our performance of religious activities. (15:22)

4. Constantly choosing not to follow a command of God is like becoming a tool in the hand of Satan. (15:23)
5. Focusing on God in a crisis gives us stability; godly actions will result. (14:1–15)
6. No matter what words we may say, our hearts will be revealed by what we do. (15:20, 24)

8

THE IMPORTANCE OF A GOD-FOCUS!

1 Samuel 16–17

How could Debbie, the young mother of two small children who attends our church, ever know how much I've learned from her?

Her life as a single parent is difficult. There are pressure-filled, discouraging, even overwhelming days. Yet, in the midst of them, I've seen her decisions to follow God's Word strengthen her children, encourage the people with whom she works, and enable her to help others in our church. Debbie has a God-focus that comes from being committed to studying God's Word and applying it to her life.

During hard times I've heard her pray, "Lord, I don't know how all this fits together in Your plan. But I believe You're telling me to go this way. And I know the only way through is to follow You."

God has not given Debbie an easy life. But He *has* given her the power to obey Him, and obeying Him gives her peace and joy.

* * * *

In 1 Samuel 16:1–4 Samuel faces a problem and responds by looking to God.

In the next chapter Israel faces a problem and responds in dismay. The difference between Samuel and Israel was one of perspective. One viewed life from the perspective of who God is and what He can do and the other from a strictly human perspective. In this lesson we will also see how *our* perspective affects *our* actions.

Cultural Insights

David's Family:

Some scholars explain that the family of Jesse, the father of David, occupied a leading place in Bethlehem, as they were known for their devoted service to the Lord. This is not surprising, since Jesse's grandparents were Ruth and Boaz. (See Ruth 4:21–22.) No doubt, Jesse learned from his grandparents the godly principles he passed down to his sons, notably David.

David's Occupation:

God's wise plans for David's life included years in the quiet seclusion of shepherd fields. God chose for His servant a humble profession that allowed time for deep meditation upon God.

This work also afforded training for emergencies in which the lonely shepherd-to-be-king had to rely on God alone to empower him to protect the flocks from lions, bears, and other dangers.

David's   A firm and unshaken trust in God. David saw
Character: God as the only true ruler in Israel; he consis-
              tently strove to reverence Israel's King and to
              follow His ways. After David's errors and
              transgressions, he showed his strong character
              in returning to the Lord all the more loyally.
              David, being a man after God's own heart,
              showed what God can do through a will sur-
              rendered to Him.

Discovery 1 / God Prepares His Man / (16:1–12)

1. Read 15:35 with 16:1. What was Samuel experiencing? Why?

   _____

   _____

   In 6:1, how does God encourage Samuel?

   _____

2. State Samuel's first response to this responsibility. (v. 2)

   _____

   How did the Lord again encourage Samuel? (vv. 2–3)

   _____

   Despite his feelings, what decision did Samuel make concerning God's command? (v. 4)

   _____

   What phrases in v. 3 indicate that Samuel would have to trust God in this venture?

   _____

   _____

3. List the specific things God did in 6:1–12 to enable Samuel to carry out his mission. (How did Samuel know where to go? How did he find the right man?)

_____

_____

Discovery 2 / An Unexpected Anointing / (16:6–13)

4. In light of vv. 6–7, 9:2, and 10:23–24, why do you think Samuel at first thought Eliab to be God's choice?

_____

_____

In contrast, what is God's criterion for those He chooses as leaders? (v. 7)

_____

_____

After reading 1 Chronicles 28:9; 2 Chronicles 16:9; and Luke 16:15, write your own definition of the phrase "the Lord looks at the heart."

_____

_____

As you reflect on these verses, what should be your primary concern? Is it your first priority?

_____

_____

5. Did David do anything to set himself up for this honor? What are David's family responsibilities? (v. 11)

_____

_____

6. What happened to David immediately after his anointing? (v. 13) Had the same thing happened to Saul? (10:1, 10)

_____

_____

7. The anointing of David took place when he was about fifteen years old. According to 2 Samuel 5:4, how many years did it take for the fact to become a reality?

_____

_____

Can you recall and describe a time when you were assured by God that something would take place, but for which you had to wait?

_____

_____

Discovery 3 / A New Training Ground / (16:14–23)

8. What has become of Saul?

_____

_____

9. As the Scripture introduces David, what character traits and abilities are emphasized?

_____

_____

What were Saul's initial feelings toward David? Why do you think Saul felt this way toward the younger man?

_____

_____

10. What preparation for kingship might these early experiences at court have given David?

_____

_____

Can you share ways God has gradually prepared you for a particular role, event, or ministry?

_____

_____

_____

Discovery 4 / Looking at the Problem / (17:1–31)

11. Israel now faces a frightening new aspect to her old problem. Write a description of their "big" problem. Briefly summarize Goliath's challenge to Israel. (vv. 4–10)

_____

_____

How did Israel respond to this challenge? (vv. 11, 24) Judging from this response, what perspective do Saul and his men seem to have had of their problem?

_____

_____

12. What incentive did Saul give his people for fighting Goliath? (v. 25) Did this motivation prompt his soldiers to action? Explain.

_____

_____

_____

13. How did God get David to the scene of battle? (vv. 12–20)

_____

_____

In contrast to Saul and his army, what does David's attitude or perspective seem to be when challenged by Goliath? (vv. 23–26) What motivation resulted? (vv. 30–32)

_____

_____

What motivates you to confront problems in your (1) personal life, (2) marriage, and (3) parent/child relationships?

1. _____

_____

2. _____

_____

3. _____

_____

Discovery 5 / Confronting the Problem / (17:32–58)

14. On what basis does Saul reason that David cannot be Israel's representative? (vv. 31–33)

_____

In what way was Saul's thinking similar to Goliath's? Compare vv. 32–33 with vv. 42–44.

_____

_____

15. As David reasons with Saul (vv. 34–37), what does he indicate he knows about God? How had God prepared David for this day? What might God be teaching you about Himself in the events of your life?

    _____

    _____

    _____

    How did David's knowledge of God affect his actions? (vv. 39–48)

    _____

16. What contrasting resources for fighting this battle are given? (v. 45) Which was most effective? (vv. 48–50)

    _____

    _____

    What is God's promise to you in Isaiah 41:10?

    _____

    As a believer in Jesus Christ, what pieces of armor are you to put on? (Eph. 6:13–17)

    _____

    _____

    In light of David's victory and a Christian's armor, as described in Ephesians 6, reflect on any battles you are now facing. Describe a specific strategy that will ensure the enemy's defeat.

    _____

    _____

    _____

17. What important truth did David want the people of God to learn? (v. 47)

   _____

   What effect did David's faith and actions have on his countrymen? (vv. 45–48)

   _____

   How might this cause-and-effect relationship apply in a family or church situation?

   _____

   _____

   (For reflection: When your desire is similar to David's here, what might family members and friends learn through you? Stop now and pray that God might make this perspective real in your heart and mind.)

*   *   *   *

Key Principles from Lesson 8

1. God will prepare us for the responsibilities to which we are called. (16:1–12)
2. Even though people look at externals, God looks at the heart. (16:7)
3. God may assure us of something through His Word long before we actually experience it. (16:13)
4. God selects just the right "training ground" for each of us, according to His plan for our life. (16:14–23) (Remember: God is evaluating your training on the basis of your heart, *not* on your performance! In new areas, such as self-discipline, reverencing your husband, or praising

your children, your performance may be weak, but if you have made the decision to be faithful to God and His commands and are trusting Him for the power to be trained, He will strongly support you. [2 Cor. 16:9] If your heart is right, you are in fact succeeding long before your performance manifests "success.")

5. When we respond in submission and in obedience to God's ongoing training, we are prepared for circumstances as they arise and for our special role or life ministry. (chapter 17)

6. A godly perspective, which comes from spending time with God in His Word and in prayer, leads to godly motivation and this results in godly action. (chapter 17)

7. You will know what a person believes by his or her actions. (17:11, 40)

8. If we have a godly perspective, we will transfer to present circumstances what God has taught us in the past. (17:31–37)

9. When confronting a problem, we need to come with a divine perspective and in the strength of the Lord, or else we will not be facing the problem correctly.

10. We influence others when we exhibit faith. (17:46–47, 52)

9

HANDLING DIFFICULTIES

1 Samuel 18–20

One morning there was a knock at the door. It was my neighbor. "Never a dull moment around our house!" she exclaimed. "As soon as one problem is gone, two more pop up!"

We sat down for a cup of coffee, and she continued. "I wake up at night and my mind's like a TV screen. I think about one problem for a while, and then say, 'Nope, let's not look at that one.' But then another problem flashes onto the screen, and then another. Soon I'm thinking of what David said, 'My soul weeps because of grief.'

"You know me . . . self-pity's my old bug-a-boo. But the Bible *is* having an effect on my life. I've had to rearrange my mornings to study the Bible, but do you know what? God *is* becoming my stronghold, just like David said!"

* * * *

This week's lesson teaches principles for handling difficulties. The Scripture passage shows that sin, left unchecked, will destroy the soul. Certainly there are terrible diseases that destroy the body, but none is so terrible as the disease that destroys the soul.

Character Insight

David
the psalmist: David reveals the inner feelings of one after God's heart. The facts of an event do not give insight into the character's emotions. However, the psalms of David do often show us his heart's deliberations over the events recorded in 1 Samuel.

David's psalms reveal that struggles, fears, and disappointments may be experienced by one who has a heart after God. At the same time, the psalms clearly declare God and His ways as the solution to problems. Consistently, David the psalmist finds refreshment, strength, and encouragement through meditating upon the character and works of his almighty God. How could David ever know that his periods of reflecting upon God and His works would minister to all future generations of believers!

Discovery 1 / A Fire Sparks / (18:1–13)

Commit your study time to the Lord. Ask Him to strengthen you and make clear His way for you.

1. Carefully reread v. 5. List everything this verse says or implies about David at court. (What is his new responsibility? What effect does it have and upon whom? and so

forth) For further insight into this verse compare 17:15 and 18:2.

_____

_____

_____

2. How would you summarize Saul's reaction (vv. 6–9) to David's success?

_____

What is God's statement in James 3:14–16 about emotions such as Saul's?

_____

What does it appear Saul did about or with his emotions?

_____

According to what God says in His Word, what can you do when tempted to react as Saul did?

1) Psalm 1:1–2 _____

2) 1 John 1:9 _____

3) Philippians 4:6–7 _____

4) Galatians 5:16 _____

Summarizing the challenge from each passage, develop a practical plan of action you (or your child) could use when tempted like Saul.

_____

_____

_____

_____

Name the actions that resulted from Saul's jealousy. (18:10–11, 13)

_____

_____

3. How does Saul finally handle his problem? (v. 13) What does such a "solution" reveal about Saul?

_____

_____

Discovery 2 / God Supports David / (18:14–19:24)

4. The unchecked fire grew inside Saul. List the evil he designed for David. Alongside each evil, describe how the Lord protected David and/or turned evil into good.

_____

_____

_____

What does the above list show about God's character? (See 1 Chronicles 16:9.)

_____

Read Proverbs 29:23. How was this maxim proven true for David? (18:18, 23)

_____

5. Describe a current situation in which you are trusting God to bring good from what looks as if it were harm or evil.

_____

_____

_____

God's Word is always the safest path to follow. Relate an instance when following God's command protected you.

_____

_____

Discovery 3 / Reaching for God / (Psalm 59)

6. First Samuel 19:9–20 relates an event in the life of David. But Psalm 59 tells what was going on *inside* of David at this time. Only in studying this psalm do we see the intensity of David's emotions.

   Read Psalm 59. In this psalm David likens the men prowling around his home to growling dogs at night.

   State David's feelings concerning his situation as reflected in the Psalm. If possible support your answer with verse references.

   _____

   _____

   _____

   Despite circumstances, what facts about God brought David hope?

   _____

   Because of his hope, what did David say he would be able to do? Support your answer with verses.

   _____

   What did David want others to learn through his deliverance?

   _____

   _____

In the end, how does David respond to his God? Reflect on the personal situation you described in question 5. In light of Psalm 59:16–17, how should you face your trouble?

_____

_____

7. What does Michal reveal about herself as she helps David escape? Are there sinful practices in our culture that at times you're tempted to resort to?

_____

_____

_____

Discovery 4 / A Faithful Friend / (1 Sam. 20:1–17)

8. Jonathan and David, close friends who loved the Lord, discussed David's situation. The two men viewed the problem differently.

How did David describe the problem? (vv. 1, 3)

_____

How did Jonathan view it? (vv. 2, 9)

_____

What test is set up to determine the truth? (vv. 5–7) What attitude toward God does such a test reflect?

_____

_____

Even though Jonathan disagreed with David, what was his consistent attitude toward him? Support your answer.

_____

_____

Name two of your closest friends. Write out a "principle of friendship" that you have learned from this passage and that you intend to follow in these two relationships.

_____

_____

_____

9. One of the most touching private conversations recorded in Scripture takes place between these two friends, Jonathan and David.

   In vv. 11–17, what does Jonathan indicate he knows about David's future? Might this have caused Jonathan to be jealous?

   _____

   _____

   Does it appear the evil of Saul's heart had influenced his son Jonathan? Explain and support your answer.

   _____

   _____

   What did Jonathan promise to do for his friend? (vv. 12–13)

   _____

   _____

10. Summarize the covenant made between Jonathan and David. What does Deuteronomy 23:21 say about the importance of covenants?

    _____

    _____

Discovery 5 / God Takes David Away / (20:18–42)

11. Whom did both David and Jonathan acknowledge as being in control of their "test of truth"? (vv. 18–22)

   _____

   _____

12. In being faithful to David, what did Jonathan risk? In what ways did God use Jonathan to help and encourage David? (vv. 24–42)

   _____

   _____

   During the test, how did God open Jonathan's eyes to the truth? (vv. 30–34)

   _____

   _____

   In being loyal to his friend, did Jonathan "tear down" his father? Support your answer.

   _____

   _____

13. Though God's direction was clear, how did David feel about leaving?

   _____

   _____

   What reasons might David have had for crying?

   _____

   _____

   _____

Can you remember a time in your life when the "arrow" fell in a direction opposite from what you had hoped? Describe your emotions. How did God encourage you?

_____

_____

_____

*   *   *   *

Key Principles from Lesson 9

1. Envy and jealousy destroy one's ability to reason. Left unchecked, they can destroy a life. (18:6–9)
2. Refusing envy and jealousy give one freedom to love and the blessings of love and loyalty. (20:1–9)
3. In any circumstance the safest road to follow is God's. (chapter 18)
4. God will defend and strongly support one who walks in His ways. (chapters 18, 19 and 2 Chron. 16:9)
5. When you focus on God and place your hope in Him, you find refuge in the day of distress. David did not deny the presence of difficulty but made a decision to concentrate upon his God instead of on the problem. (Ps. 59)
6. God's will is not always pleasant, but it *is* the path to blessing. (chapter 20)
7. God supplies the encouragement we need to follow His ways. (20:40–42)

10

WAITING ON GOD

1 Samuel 21–24

After Tom and Pat led Sandy, a drug pusher and someone who had "done time" in a reformatory, to the Lord, they invited her to live with them and their children for a while. They quickly learned that this resulted in two worlds crashing together. It was very difficult for Sandy to feel comfortable with family life and with the love expressed there. And it was equally difficult for her new family to cope with her behavior when it showed the effects of the angry, violent, rebellious world that had been hers since childhood.

At times, in the high emotion and intensity of their situation, Tom, Pat and Sandy could lose sight of God's love and faithfulness. At times, they felt overwhelmed.

At such times a quick escape from the stress looked good to Tom and Pat, but, long before Sandy had moved into their home, God had taught them the importance of waiting on Him. They had learned that a "light at the end of the tunnel" that was not God's light brought only frustration and misery. So they prayed:

"Lord, we know that the right way in this situation is Your way, so please give us strength to wait on You. And help our trusting You to encourage both our children and Sandy."

* * * *

In our impatient, instant-everything society, waiting on God is not easy. We often picture waiting as something passive, much like twiddling our thumbs. But waiting on God is intensely *active*. It requires us to "trust in the LORD with all [our] heart and lean not on [our] own understanding" (Prov. 3:5).

In several difficult situations in this lesson David learns to wait on God. And we in turn learn from David.

Cultural Insight

Nob: A city in the tribe of Benjamin. It was set on a hill and was very near Jerusalem. David often stopped here before embarking on some dangerous undertaking for King Saul. It is not known for certain if the tabernacle was located here at the time of the events in our lesson.

Discovery 1 / The Pressure Is On / (21:1–9)

1. According to the passage, what did David need from Ahimelech?

_____

Did David give Ahimelech accurate reasons for his coming to Nob? Explain. What does this indicate about David's reliance upon God at this point?

_____

_____

In light of Proverbs 6:16–17, how did God feel about David's explanation to the priest?

_____

2. In order to discover the heart attitude of the priest toward David consider the following:

The law (Lev. 24:5–9) allowed the priests to eat the holy bread after it had been offered to the Lord. What did Ahimelech choose to do with the bread that was to have been his?

_____

What major contrast do you see between the heart attitudes of David and the priest?

_____

3. The Scripture takes special note that this encounter was observed. Who was this observer? (v. 7)

_____

What lessons might be learned from David's encounter with Ahimelech?

_____

_____

Discovery 2 / David is Delivered / (1 Sam. 21:10–15; Pss. 56 and 34)

4. How would you describe David's experience at the Philistine city of Gath? (21:10–15)

_____

_____

_____

5. Psalm 56 gives us a glimpse into David's heart when he was in Gath.

   Read the psalm and then list David's feelings concerning his circumstances. (Cite verse references supporting your findings.)

   _____

   _____

   Which phrases in the Psalm particularly indicate how much God cares for David?

   _____

   _____

   What is the overall focus of David's psalm?

   _____

   _____

   List the conclusions David came to because of this focus.

   _____

   _____

   Uncover at least two principles in this Psalm. Relate each to a specific situation in your life.

   1. _____

   _____

   2. _____

   _____

6. Psalm 56 reveals David's thoughts during his dangerous visit to Gath, but Psalm 34 lets us in on David's feelings *after* his deliverance.

Read Psalm 34. To what or whom does David attribute his deliverance? Support your answer by listing some of the verses that speak of deliverance.

_____

_____

_____

What does this psalm say about God's protection of His children?

_____

_____

_____

What does David say he will do because God protects and delivers? (vv. 1–3)

_____

_____

List some ways you are in need of protection. Apply two of the truths in Psalm 34 to specific needs in your life.

_____

_____

_____

_____

_____

According to this psalm, what should a woman who wants a long life remember to do? (vv. 12–14)

_____

_____

Discovery 3 / The Sad Results of Expediency / (1 Sam. 22)

7. Describe the type of men God gathered around David. (vv. 1–2) What training would leading such a group give David?

_____

_____

_____

What adjustments might this new life as a fugitive have forced upon David?

_____

8. What aspects of David's character are revealed in vv. 3–5? Which of these characteristics are of special challenge to your life and why?

_____

_____

_____

9. In strong contrast to David, what attitudes of Saul do vv. 6–8 describe?

_____

_____

To what type of individual did Saul listen? (vv. 9–10) (See also Ps. 1:1–2.)

_____

Allowed to go unchecked, what did Saul's attitudes and ungodly conclusions ultimately lead him to do?

_____

_____

10. How did David respond to news of the tragedy in Nob?

_____

What important lesson might David have learned from this tragedy and his involvement in it?

_____

Discovery 4 / Saul Pursues David / (Chapter 23)

11. David wanted to help his countrymen at Keilah. What was his first step in the process? (vv. 1–2)

_____

What important principle is shown here? In what way might you follow David's example this coming week?

_____

_____

_____

12. In v. 3 did David's men struggle to accept God's will? Why?

_____

What might David's men have learned from their battle at Keilah?

_____

Though David had helped the people of Keilah, what sad truth did he have to face? (vv. 7–13) What did David do when he realized what might soon happen?

_____

_____

_____

13. What phrase in 23:14 illustrates God's sovereign control?

_____

14. When David was tired and discouraged what did God do? (vv. 16–18)

_____

What phrase indicates the main purpose of Jonathan's visit?

_____

What rare character traits does Saul's son display?

_____

15. Who besides Saul was causing David hardship? (vv. 19–24) Why would this treachery have been difficult for David to face?

_____

_____

Describe the severity of the situation shown in vv. 25–26.

_____

_____

16. When hope of deliverance was almost gone, what did God do? (v. 27)

_____

_____

What application do you see here for life?

_____

_____

17. Psalm 54 also describes this event. What is suggested here as the reason the people of Ziph turned against David?

_____

What hope did David express in this Psalm?

_____

Apply this same hope to a circumstance you are facing as a wife, mother, or single woman.

_____

_____

Discovery 5 / **David Waits on God** / (Chapter 24)

18. Read 1 Samuel 24:1–7. What situation arose that seemed to provide a way of escape for David?

_____

What did David's men encourage him to do? What did they use to try to influence him?

_____

_____

How did David react to their suggestion?

_____

19. Read 1 Samuel 24:8–22. Through David, God attempted to bring Saul to repentance. State two godly attitudes David exhibits in his emotional plea to Saul.

_____

_____

_____

List the temporary effects of David's unselfishness upon Saul.

_____

_____

_____

20. In what area of your life do you need to wait on God? What truths in chapters 21–24 either encourage you or teach you how to wait on God? Relate these truths to your specific circumstance.

_____

_____

_____

_____

_____

_____

_____

*   *   *   *

Key Principles from Lesson 10

1. Desperate situations are not an excuse for compromising the commands of God. (21:1–9)
2. Sin always affects others. (22:9–20; Ps. 54:3)
3. Before helping others, it is wise to ask the Lord which course of action will be more beneficial. (23:1–5)
4. God alone is our refuge and protection. Though our circumstances change, God remains the same. (Ps. 56:3; 1 Sam. 21; 23:26–28)

5. If we who desire to follow God's commands ask Him for help, He always answers. (Ps. 34)
6. A good life comes to those who speak truth, depart from evil and do good, and pursue peace. (Ps. 34:13–14)
7. When we grow weary of following after God, He brings encouragement. (23:16–18)
8. We are not to take things into our own hands, but wait upon God to deliver us from our difficulties. (chapter 24)

11

INJUSTICE AND REVENGE

1 Samuel 25–27

It was the second time Ruth's husband had been cheated out of a business he had started. Thousands of dollars that should have gone to him had been used by his partners. Walking through the beautiful new home of one of the men who had wronged her husband, Ruth was filled with bitterness and resentment.

"It makes me so mad," she confided later to her daughter. "That home was bought and furnished with our money! . . . It's not fair! . . . I'll never forgive them."

*   *   *   *

How to cope with the hurt of injustice is a difficult issue—in any age. The situations in this lesson will be very practical for each person studying this lesson, because all of us have experienced injustice, as well as the resulting bondage of resentment.

Cultural Insights

Robbers: Roving bands of robbers were very common in the Wilderness of Paran, where David fled after Samuel died. Even to the present day, groups of men protect the life and property of wilderness dwellers in return for gifts. Even during David's most difficult times, he took upon himself the care and protection of his countrymen.

Bound in the Bundle of the Living: A Hebrew saying, referring to life beyond the grave. It is often found on Jewish tombstones, even recent ones. The image comes from the custom of bundling valuable possessions to prevent them from being broken or damaged. It is a picture of a precious jewel, carefully tied up to keep it secure and safe.

Discovery 1 / A Husband and Wife / (Chapter 25)

As you study consider: "Your statutes are my delight; they are my counselors" (Ps. 119:24).

"Then Samuel died." Chapter 25 begins with what must have been a very emotional time for Israel. Samuel was dead. All Israel mourned the loss of a great man of God. Samuel had been the link between two very different forms of government—judges and kings. He was the last spokesman of an era that would never return. Samuel had been born in Ramah, had administered the affairs of Israel from that city, and at the last was buried there.

1. As fully and as accurately as possible, describe Nabal.

_____

_____

In light of Proverbs 12:15–16; 13:16, what actions of Nabal's indicated he was a fool?

_____

2. Describe and characterize Nabal's wife, Abigail. Give verse references to support your answer.

_____

_____

_____

3. What sharp contrast do you see between Nabal's and Abigail's view of David? (vv. 10–11, 28–30)

_____

_____

4. What kind of reputation did David's men have among the shepherds? (vv. 14–16)

_____

How do your neighbors describe you and your family?

_____

_____

_____

5. Why did David quickly put on his sword? (v. 13)

_____

_____

In a dictionary look up the word "revenge," and write out a brief definition of your own.

_____

_____

In light of your definition, what do you think David was feeling at this time?

_____

_____

Discovery 2 / Abigail Meets David / (25:18–44)

6. When Abigail heard the shepherd's report, how did she respond?

_____

In v. 34 what did David say about the importance of Abigail's actions?

_____

Do you think what Abigail did was dangerous? Why or why not?

_____

7. When Abigail told David he would be "bound in the bundle of the living," what was she trying to get him to see? (See Cultural Insight.) In contrast, what does she say will happen to David's enemies?

_____

_____

_____

What three things did Abigail humbly ask David to consider? (vv. 23–31)

_____

_____

_____

_____

8. The Lord used Abigail to help David learn what important lesson?

   _____

   What would have happened to David if he had carried out his planned attack? (vv. 30–33)

   _____

   _____

   In light of this passage, why do you think God said that vengeance is His?

   _____

   _____

   Through Abigail God taught David a lesson. Think of your own situation. How might Abigail's wisdom prevent you from repaying evil with evil? Be specific.

   _____

   _____

9. What does David's response to Abigail show about a person after God's heart?

   _____

   _____

10. As you review Chapter 25:

    List the ways God protected and made provision for David.

    _____

    _____

    _____

    _____

List ways God protected and provided for Abigail.

_____

_____

_____

_____

Show other ways God's sovereign control over all things is demonstrated in this chapter. Support your answer with verse references. In what ways are you encouraged by the story of Nabal, Abigail, and David?

_____

_____

_____

_____

Discovery 3 / David Remembers / (26:1–12)

11. What cruel step had Saul taken to sever all ties with David? (25:44)

_____

Once again the Ziphites secured Saul's favor by disclosing David's hiding place. In chapter 26 how did David apply the lesson God had taught him through Abigail and the lesson recorded in 24:4–6?

_____

_____

As they worked together, what did David teach Abishai? (vv. 9–10)

_____

_____

(Stop and ask the Lord to help *you* be sensitive to times when you can teach a child a lesson you have learned from 1 Samuel. Share such a teaching insight in your group.)

12. What phrase in v. 12 gives the clue that the Lord was responsible for testing David and Abishai?

_____

_____

Discovery 4 / David and Saul / (26:13–25)

13. Through actions and words, what did David try to tell Saul? List the specific statements that prove David's point.

_____

_____

_____

How did David's plea appear to affect Saul? What did Saul admit? Do you think Saul was sincere? Explain.

_____

_____

_____

Discovery 5 / David Despairs / (Chapter 27)

14. After living in difficult circumstances for quite some time, what three conclusions does David draw? (v. 1)

_____

_____

_____

In light of David's previous assurances as recorded in Psalms 34, 54, 56, and 59, what do you think was happening to him? Compare his present approach to securing safety with what is recorded in Psalm 56.

_____

_____

_____

_____

Relate a personal experience where you came to a conclusion similar to David's. Were you trusting the Lord for his direction?

_____

_____

_____

15. How does the enemy king receive David? What does he expect of David? (Especially consider the strong statement of v. 12.)

_____

_____

How long did David stay in fellowship with the enemy? (v. 7)

_____

_____

How would you describe David's actions during this time?

_____

_____

Formulate one principle for living which you discovered in chapter 27.

_____

_____

*   *   *   *

Key Principles from Lesson 11

1. If we consistently practice or have a heart to practice the principles of God, we will be prepared to make wise and scriptural decisions in times of emergency. (Chapter 25)
2. If we are prepared to make wise decisions, we are not likely to become bewildered or confused in difficult circumstances. (25:20)
3. We are *not* to avenge ourself by our own hand. (25:31, 33)
4. Being vengeful will cause us grief and a troubled heart. (25:31)
5. Those who are secure in the Lord and desire His will, are able to receive reproof or correction. (25:32–34.)
6. The awareness that God's children are "bound in the bundle of the living" produces security.
7. Conclusions and actions based on our circumstances alone—apart from the truths of Scripture—can lead us along a dangerous, wayward path. (Chapter 27)

12

DILEMMAS AND CRISES

1 Samuel 28–30

Diane couldn't believe it when her husband told her he wanted a divorce. She felt shocked and horrified when she thought about being divorced, and she felt very uncertain about the future.

"What do I do now?" she asked.

In the midst of a crisis, when we feel overwhelmed and our thoughts are confused, knowing where to turn and then doing it can give us both stability and comfort. However, turning to the wrong person or thing can be destructive.

*   *   *   *

In this lesson we view the struggles of David and Saul, two people in crisis. David turns to God, Saul to that which is condemned by God. For Saul, as for many today, compromising God's commands looked like the easier way, but in the end greater difficulties resulted.

Cultural Insight

Witchcraft: An important part of the various Canaanite pagan religions. If one's daughter was a witch, she was, of all women, most "blessed."

After the Israelites had fled Egypt and entered the Promised Land, God commanded them to drive out the Canaanites. Several hundred years later, in the time of David and Saul, we see one of the results of Israel's failure to obey God's command: witchcraft was still being practiced in the land, tempting the people not to trust in God.

Discovery 1 / David's Dilemma / (28:1–2; 1 Chron. 12:1–22)

1. First Chronicles 12 describes David's circumstances during his self-imposed exile in the land of the Philistines. What does 1 Chronicles 12:22 say began to happen? What effect might this have had on David?

_____

_____

_____

According to 1 Chronicles 12:8 what kind of men were defecting to David's camp? What did they know about David? (v. 8)

_____

_____

With what attitude did David receive them? (1 Chron. 12:17–18)

_____

2. Into what corner did David's retreat into "safety" get both him and his men? (1 Sam. 28:1–2)

_____

_____

What anxieties do you think this turn of events may have caused David and his followers?

_____

_____

What principle for living can you discover here?

_____

_____

Discovery 2 / Saul's Dilemma / (28:3–10)

3. What two facts are noted in v. 3?

_____

_____

4. List Saul's responses to the stress of an imminent Philistine attack. (vv. 5–8)

_____

_____

_____

5. The Word of God is very specific about witches and mediums. How does God view any form of the occult? (Deut. 18:9–12; Rev. 21:8)

_____

_____

_____

In light of God's attitude, how should we respond to various occult activities? What modern-day forms might the occult take?

_____

_____

6. What paradox appears in vv. 3 and 7–10? What does this contradiction reveal about Saul's character?

_____

_____

Can you think of and describe areas of your life in which you say one thing and do the opposite?

_____

_____

Discovery 3 / Unwelcome Words / (28:11–25)

7. Why do you think Saul so *desperately* wanted to talk with Samuel?

_____

8. When the witch saw Samuel, why was she so amazed? (vv. 11–13)

_____

List at least three ways Samuel's message was consistent with his prophecies and teachings when alive on earth. (See 1 Samuel 13:13; 15:22–29.)

_____

_____

_____

_____

9. Though Saul claimed he wanted instruction from Samuel, how had he responded to such advice in the past?

_____

Instead of telling Saul what to do, what information does Samuel offer? (v. 19)

_____

Why was Saul to lose his life? (1 Chron. 10:13–14)

_____

What was the attitude of Saul's response to Samuel's message? Do you see any repentance on Saul's part?

_____

_____

10. What do you learn about God through Saul's experience at Endor?

_____

_____

Discovery 4 / God Is Faithful / (29:1–30:19)

11. Whom did God use to help David out of the "impossible" dilemma of fighting against his own people? How was this "deliverance" accomplished?

_____

_____

How would you account for David's seemingly treasonous words in 29:8?

_____

_____

In 29:9, with what interesting term did Achish describe David?

_____

_____

12. Another "impossible" situation confronted David almost immediately. Name at least four specific sorrows David faced when he returned to Ziklag. (30:1–6)

_____

_____

_____

_____

What phrase in 30:1–8 tells how David was strengthened in his sorrow?

_____

_____

What does this phrase mean to you?

_____

_____

Which phrase best explains how David discovered what to do in this crisis?

_____

_____

When you are in difficulty, how or in what do you find comfort and direction?

_____

_____

13. How *specific* was David's prayer? (vv. 7–8)

_____

How *specific* was God's answer? (v. 8)

_____

What response did David have to God's instructions? (vv. 9–19)

_____

_____

List the ways in which God, in this victory, had proved faithful to His promises to David.

_____

_____

_____

Discovery 5 / David, A Wise Leader / (30:20–31)

14. What principle did David try to teach his men?

_____

_____

Who might you want to reward for their past deeds and loyalty? How might you go about this?

_____

_____

_____

How does Scripture describe the complaining men?

_____

_____

15. What does David do in vv. 26–31, and how might his actions be a model for your family to follow? Be specific in your application.

_____

_____

_____

*   *   *   *

Key Principles from Lesson 12

1. When we compromise we can get caught in traps. (Chapters 27 and 29)
2. We are to have *nothing* to do with any form of witch-craft. (28:3–10)
3. In crisis, hurt, or sorrow, we should first turn to the Lord for comfort and direction. (30:6, 8)
4. In every difficulty (even those we may bring upon ourselves) God will help us, *if* we turn to Him in humility. (Chapters 29 and 30)
5. When God richly blesses you remember those who have, in the past, helped you. (30:20–31)

13

REALIZING GOD'S FAITHFULNESS

1 Samuel 31

The first time I taught the Book of First Samuel, God was leading me through one of the most difficult times of my life. God graciously used this book of the Bible to impress upon my mind the principle of having a heart after Him, no matter what the circumstances.

Some years later, as I was preparing these lessons for publication, I reflected on God's faithfulness to me then.

"Lord, I praise you for sustaining me with your faithfulness and power in my difficulties.

"You were faithful to David, and You've been faithful to me too. Just when I felt I couldn't live one more day in my circumstances, I found that waiting on You was the shortest route to blessing.

"You know my struggles, Lord, and You know there were falls. Yet in every circumstance You were in control!

"I realize now, my wise Father, that you were faithfully answering my question as to what a heart after Yours really is.

I've learned that You are not interested in performance, but in my heart attitude. David's words in Psalm 19:14 have new meaning for me now: 'May the words of my mouth and the meditation of my heart be pleasing in your sight, O LORD, my Rock and my Redeemer.' "

* * * *

This final lesson in our study deals with the last chapter in First Samuel. And this also ushers in a new era in David's life: his rule as king. God goes on to complete the work He began in David long before, a work that stretches down through the ages by means of David's psalms and the record of his life focused in the Bible.

Cultural Insight

Philistines: When Saul's anger forced David to flee, Israel lost her best military leader. As long as David led the army, the Philistines were held back. But with David gone, the Philistines began to be more and more bold in their infiltration.

During his last years as king, Saul and his army spent most of their time trying to capture David rather than defending Israel. Thus the Philistines prepared once again for a major battle, confident of victory over Saul and his weakened army.

Chapter 31 describes the Philistines' third major attack on Israel. The first wave had been stopped by Samuel at the battle of Ebenezer (7:13). The second major attack had been curtailed by Saul at the battle of Micmash (14:31).

Discovery 1 / The Fateful Battle / (31:1–6)

1. Step back in time and write a brief summary of the famous battle described in chapter 31. (Use a separate sheet of paper. You might try writing your summary from the viewpoint of Saul's armor-bearer.)

2. What phrases in 28:19 indicate who was responsible for this battle's outcome?

   _____

   What do you think their defeat indicated to the Israelites? (Compare today's passage with 7:3–4, 13.)

   _____

   God blessed Israel with victory over her enemies when she had a heart to walk in His ways, but enemies overpowered her when the Lord was forsaken. Ask God to help you explain this principle to a child. In your group, share the approach you took in your explanation.

   _____

   _____

Discovery 2 / Picking Up the Pieces / (31:7–13)

3. What do the actions of the Philistines *after* the battle indicate about their character? (vv. 7–10)

   _____

   How do the actions of the people of Jabesh-gilead demonstrate their character? Why might the men of Jabesh-gilead have responded in such a way?

   _____

   _____

   _____

Discovery 3 / The Tragic Report / (2 Samuel 1:1–16)

4. On the third day after the battle David hears of it. How has the story changed? Why might this solider have fabricated such a story? What did his deception cost him? What did the young man obviously not understand about David? (See 1 Sam. 26:9–11 for insight.)

5. What was David's immediate response to the news, and why might such a reaction be unusual? As you recall what you have learned about David, was this reaction out of character? Explain.

Discovery 4 / David's Lament / (2 Sam. 1:17–27)

David's lament, or chant over Saul and Jonathan, became known as the "Song of the Bow." It seems David had a custom of teaching military music to encourage spirit among his men, and this lament was added to the selections.

6. In his song what mention did David make of his trials or painful relations with Saul? What does this indicate to you?

_____

_____

_____

What does David emphasize about Saul's life?

_____

What tribute does he give Jonathan?

_____

Discovery 5 / Conclusions and Goals

7. State three things that stood out to you about David's responses during his difficult days of exile, giving an

example for each. Name one specific lesson you learned from David that has helped you in your difficulties. Briefly explain.

_____

_____

_____

_____

_____

8. Name four individuals in 1 Samuel who focused on God instead of their circumstances. Give an example when each did so.

_____

_____

_____

_____

9. What have you learned about God that would encourage you to focus upon who He is and what He can do—no matter what your circumstances.

_____

_____

_____

In what ways have you already begun to do this?

_____

_____

_____

_____

10. Now what do you think it means to be after God's heart?

_____

_____

11. Write out three specific goals for your future or conclusions of your present life. Commit these right now to God; who "does exceedingly abundant above all we could ask or think." Be prepared to share these goals with your group. At the end of your group discussion pray specifically for at least one goal of each person.

_____

_____

_____

*   *   *   *

Key Principles from Lesson 13

1. God is always faithful to perform His Word. (28:19; 31:1–4)
2. When we have a heart to walk in obedience to God's ways He blesses our lives; when we forsake the Lord and His ways, enemies overpower us. (7:3–4; 28:18–19)
3. Lying to "get ahead" is foolish. (2 Sam. 1:1–16)
4. We are always to show respect to God's appointed authorities (wives to husbands, employees to employers, citizens to government officials). (2 Sam. 1:14)